Martin Classical Lectures

* Out of print.

Martin Classical Lectures

Volume XXIII

The Martin Classical Lectures are delivered annually
at Oberlin College on a foundation established
by his many friends in honor of Charles Beebe Martin,
for forty-five years a teacher of classical literature
and classical art in Oberlin.

The Athenian Aristocracy
399 to 31 B.C.

Paul MacKendrick

Published for Oberlin College
By Harvard University Press
Cambridge, Massachusetts

For Sterling Dow and Benjamin D. Meritt

Preface

We know the names of some sixty-five of the *gene* to which the Athenian aristocracy belonged. Some of the names are familiar: Alkmaionidai, Philaidai, Eumolpidai; some not: Phytalidai, Eteoboutadai, Lykomidai. The Athenian system of nomenclature, unlike the Roman, concealed membership in gene, but we know incidentally the gentile affiliation of many famous Athenians and can infer other memberships, as this study attempts to show. Among the familiar *gennetai* who figure in Athenian history before 399 B.C. are Solon, Hippokleides who danced away his marriage, Peisistratos, Harmodios and Aristogeiton, Miltiades, Themistokles, Aristeides, Kimon, Xanthippos, Perikles, Thoukydides the son of Melesias, Thoukydides the historian, and Alkibiades.

The *genos* to which any one of these famous Athenians belonged was, in the words of W. S. Ferguson (*Hesperia*, 7 [1928] 24), "a closed body of well-to-do citizens, open only to the legitimate children of its members. It had a pedigree, reconstructed in a single line from a mythical ancestor down to a certain point; from that point, . . . the point of its organization, the stemma was a demonstrable reality for the various families of which it was composed, but not for their assumed interrelations, which were usually purely fictitious." A genos had common religious rites, burial places, and property; it had an archon and a treasurer; it recognized mutual rights of succession to property, and reciprocal obligations of help, defense, and redress of injury; intermarriage with other gene kept it strong. There are interesting analogies in Scots clans and Iroquois Indian tribes.

Ostensibly, after the reforms of Kleisthenes the only connection the gene had with the state was a religious one, performing for the state the rites hereditary in the genos (the Eumolpids at Eleusis), but this study attempts to demonstrate that the gennetai were able to transform religious prominence into political influence, supplying

archons, generals, moneyers, and the like, generations after
Kleisthenes, according to the handbooks, had broken their
power forever. To take only two examples. In the fourth
century the gennetes Lykourgos held high financial office
in Athens, and was a greater builder in the tradition of
the gennetai Peisistratos, Kimon, and Perikles. And in the
second century, aristocratic mint-magistrates stamped on
their coins the same symbols their ancestors had used in
the sixth. Aristocratic activities like competition in the
games, exploitation of the mines, and dynastic intermar-
riages continued unabated. This seemed to me a phenom-
enon worth study.

My interest in the Athenian aristocracy was first aroused
by Sterling Dow, who thirty years ago in a Harvard semi-
nar set me to work on the *ergastinai* inscriptions, *IG* II,[2]
1034 and 1036. In 1938 my dissertation, *de gente Attica
Eumolpidarum,* took a genos for its subject. Since then I
have pursued the theme in seminars of my own at the University of Wisconsin; in private study (generously subsidized by the University of Wisconsin Graduate School)
in the Epigraphical Museum and the American School of
Classical Studies in Athens; and, by much appreciated
invitation, at the Institute for Advanced Study at Princeton. Chapter 2 was written in the American Academy in
Rome, and Chapter 3 at the University of Ibadan, Nigeria.
In 1966 Professor Charles T. Murphy of Oberlin College
honored me with an invitation to deliver the Martin Classical Lectures there. From those lectures came this book.

I am indebted to the persons and institutions named
above, and not least to Professor Murphy for the warm
hospitality extended to me at Oberlin, and for careful
reading and criticism of my manuscript, in which his colleague Professor Nathan Greenberg joined, to the great
improvement of the text. I have had, too, the advantage
of the critical acumen of my colleague Emmett L. Ben-
nett, Jr., for which I am grateful. None of these gentlemen
is, of course, responsible for the errors which remain. But
my deepest obligation is to Sterling Dow for having started

me off, and to B. D. Meritt for having thrown open to me the wealth of documentation available at the Institute in Princeton. To these two great epigraphists I dedicate this study; I wish profoundly that it were worthier of them both.

Contents

'Ο πλοῦτος εὐρυσθενής,
ὅταν τις ἀρετᾷ κεκραμένον καθαρᾷ
βροτήσιος ἀνὴρ πότμου παραδόντος αὐτὸν ἀνάγη
πολύφιλον ἑπέταν.

Pind. *Pyth.* V, 1–4

The strength of wealth is wide,
When a mortal man
Has it from Fortune's hands, and mixes with it
An unstained nobleness, and, whom it follows,
Many are his friends.

C. M. Bowra, *Pindar* (Oxford 1964) 102

One

From the Cup of Hemlock to the Poisoned Pen
(399–322)

When Sokrates drank the hemlock in 399, Athens was under the heel of Sparta. When Demosthenes committed suicide in 322, she was under the heel of Macedon. It will be the business of this chapter to assess the part played along this Via Dolorosa by members of the aristocratic clans. Of the great names of this century the half-Medontid Plato and the Philaid Epikouros (neither of whom ever held public office), the orator Lykourgos, and perhaps Demosthenes are attested *gennetai*. Isokrates was wealthy but if he belonged to a *genos* we cannot name it; Aristotle was an alien.

Between 429 and 399, the Athenian aristocracy, decimated and depressed by the plague and elbowed aside by a nouveau-riche ruling class, largely withdrew from politics. Political apathy was now elevated into a virtue: a client of Lysias boasted (388/7), ''I am now thirty years old, . . . and, though I live near the Agora, I have never once been seen either in law-court or in council-chamber,'' [1] and on the very eve of the battle of Chaironeia, a man of pedigree uses of himself the word *apragmon,* ''politically inactive,'' [2] as a term of praise. The ideal—holding high office, contributing generously, discharging liturgies magnificently [3]—was more honored in the breach than the observance by fourth-century Athenian aristocrats. It was an age of nouveaux riches. We know of several long pedigrees, but their owners have no background of officeholding. The rich preferred property to glory: the richest man of his time, Dikaiogenes I of Anaphlystos, had a Proxenos,[4] a Gephyraios, a descendant of the tyrant-slayers Harmodios and Aristogeiton, for a son-in-law, but the son-in-law preferred pelf to the traditional duties of pedigree, even though the pedigree would help in amassing the pelf, because the Gephyraioi, or the eldest in each generation, were tax-exempt.[5] Proxenos' son, Harmodios II, was involved in an aristocratic feud with the general Iphikrates (as we shall see). Harmodios II's son Proxenos II served as general, not without vicissitudes—before 343 he was condemned and fined by the Areiopagos on an unknown charge—and fought in the final battle at Chaironeia. Another member of the genos, Demokrates of Aphidna, was pro-Macedonian, gloating over the city's misfortunes every day and feeding at the city's expense every evening: tolerance of genos prerogatives could scarcely go further.

This family's prosperity lasted at least one more generation: Proxenos II's son Harmodios III was creditor on a mortgage about 330.[6] But the great general Timotheos, a Keryx, had to borrow rugs, cloaks, and silver bowls when he wanted to entertain.[7] A descendant of Aristeides became a public charge,[8] and Demosthenes records a proud Eteoboutad indicted and executed for sitting as a three-obol juryman when he was in debt to the public treasury.[9]

Meanwhile, according to their enemies the nouveaux riches consumed and wasted conspicuously with the fruits of public graft.[10] The orators descant upon the sumptuousness of the new private houses, as contrasted with the simplicity of Aristeides, Perikles, or Miltiades.[11] The young men, pretending a Spartan simplicity, behave like hooligans, beating up honest citizens, and then, flapping their elbows against their sides like wings, imitating fighting-cocks that have won a battle.[12] Money-lenders "walk fast, talk loud, and carry a cane";[13] mistresses decked out in gold and fine raiment make flaunting sorties in state.[14] And though the rich pretend enmity in public, in private they dine and sacrifice together, sharing their profits.[15] Charges equally scandalous had been leveled against a genuine aristocrat like Alkibiades, but at least according to his selfish lights he served the state; the nouveaux riches simply lined their pocketbooks. And the aristocrats of this generation, with the notable but mostly minor exceptions which will be the subject of this chapter, kept to their attenuated estates and were, like Epikouros, for peace at any price.[16]

The Nouveaux Riches

But neither all the aristocracy nor all the nouveaux riches were irresponsible in this century. Among the aristocracy war and revolution had decimated the ranks, political apathy was a reality, and economic necessity dictated the selling off of estates on which political influence had depended. The fourth century saw the addition of a new segment to the ruling class, of the well-to-do of good but not pedigreed family. Careful studies of epigraphic evidence have shown that in the fourth century some twelve per cent of the members of the Boule were rich, and nearly half the known generals, ambassadors, and movers of decrees, and a sizable percentage of the boards of arbitrators, naval and finance boards, local bigwigs (demarchs), and superintendents and treasurers of temples and cults. There are so many cases of fathers and sons who were both generals that one can speak of a military aristocracy, as in nineteenth-century Prussia.[17] Isokrates, writing in 339, speaks of precisely this monopoly of generalships, ambassadorships, and leading administrative posts, but he does not recognize it in his own time: he relegates it to an idealized past and assigns it to "the best, the wisest, those who lived the noblest lives."[18]

The political influence of the propertied class was not diminished, but it was in part a different propertied class—an *haute bourgeoisie* instead of an aristocracy, without the flair or the sense of tradition that had animated Kleisthenes, Kimon, or Perikles, without the quick-tempered, overweening, jealous ambition of an Alkibiades.[19] The most valuable estates recorded in Athenian history (worth between two and two and a half talents) belong to the early years of this century, but their owner is the founder of his own genos, Bouselos of the Bouselidai,[20] and a long inscription of about 396/5 records the Demotionidai,[21] an aristocratic corporation within the deme Dekeleia, so obscure that con-

troversy rages as to whether it was a clan or a phratry
(the modern equivalent of the phratry being the ecclesias-
tical parish). Its function is an exclusive one: to test claims
to membership and keep out intruders, to interpret the
statute book of the phratry, to act in short like the archaic
Areiopagos on a small scale. The Demotionidai have priestly
functions and religious competence. The inscription is
valuable because from it we can extrapolate two generalizations, one about the residual uses of an aristocracy with
religious functions in a bourgeois and secular—but not anti-
clerical—state, and the other about what the powers of the
aristocracy had been in seventh-century Athens.

Aristocrats as Depicted by the Orators

Much of the evidence for the aristocracy in fourth-
century Athens comes from the orators and has to be used
with caution, since their aim is not truth but persuasion.
A pair of speeches involving the son of the famous Alkibiades illustrates attacks on the aristocracy and how they
were parried.[22] About 397 Isokrates wrote young Alkibiades' defense in a damage suit over his father's alleged theft
from the plaintiff Teisias of a team of horses. All the
arguments marshaled to convince the jury turn on prestige:
of Olympic victories, horse-racing, dynastic marriages, and
of the antityrannical stand of Alkibiades' sixth-century
Alkmaionid ancestors.[23] Lysias, charging the same young
man with desertion (395) before a court martial, attempts
to create prejudice by alleging that it is monstrous that
gennetai, because of their birth, can commit murder, incest,
and impiety with impunity, and he argues that because
young Alkibiades' ancestors had been ostracized, he is a
hereditary enemy of the state.[24]

A much more attractive young aristocrat—of unknown
genos—is Mantitheos, for whom Lysias wrote (*ca.* 390) a
defense against the charge of collaboration with the
Thirty.[25] The youngster shows an aristocratic but not un-

attractive "confident pride in his private behavior, his military career, and his political ambitions" [26]—he is not apathetic: he served in the Boule; [27] his son Mantias made money out of the silver-mines, was treasurer for the dockyards (377/6) and probably served as admiral (360/59). His grandsons, like many in this century, were involved in a tangle of unsavory litigation. Mantitheos, Lysias' client, had, like the Philaidai, useful connections with royal houses abroad and was able to live out the Thirty's reign of terror in the Crimea. Though impoverished, he was, he ingenuously admits, generous, about dowries for his sisters and about sharing his patrimony with his brother—aristocratic solidarity at its rare best; also, with aristocratic paternalism, he subsidized certain needy rankers in his battalion. He repudiates any association with the dicing and drinking of the *jeunesse dorée,* and he points with pride to his clean court record, his bravery in war, and his ancestral tradition of public service. "You ought not," he tells the Boule, "to take a man's wearing his hair long as a reason for hating him." [28]

Another aristocratic genos of which we continue to hear something is the Kerykes, and especially the Kallias-Hipponikos branch, riven as it was by feud. Kallias III,[29] the son of Alkibiades' rich father-in-law Hipponikos, was incensed over a lawsuit with the orator Andokides, his putative fellow clansman. In 399 Kallias involved him in a trial for his life; Andokides' successful defense survives.[30] Kallias inherited the office of torchbearer at the Eleusinian Mysteries and served as general with the more famous Iphikrates in the Corinthian War in 391/0. (Iphikrates' brother Teisias dedicated, about 350, an altar to Herakles, with the help of members of the genos of Praxiergidai.[31] If Teisias was a Praxiergid himself, then so was Iphikrates, and the catalogue of gennetai for the fourth century is enriched by a distinguished figure, a successful general who married a Thracian princess and was adopted by King Amyntas III of Macedonia. Iphikrates' career offers another example of aristocratic feud: when honors were proposed for him in 371/0, the Gephyraios Harmodios II, son of Proxenos of Aphidna, opposed them.) Kallias and Iphikrates beat the Spartans, which did not prevent Kallias from acting as their *proxenos* and serving on several embassies to Sparta, one of which signed a peace treaty in 371/0. He entertained philosophers in his house, including Protagoras, Gorgias, Prodikos, Hippias, and Sokrates. He was a throwback to the great old days when the aristocracy flourished, but he died poor.[32]

Another aristocratic general in the Corinthian war was Demainetos of Paiania, a Bouzyges.[33] Since he probably came from the same deme as the famous Demosthenes, and since the name Demosthenes, which is surprisingly rare, occurs in his family, they were probably related; thus we have some slight grounds for claiming the orator as a Bouzyges.

In 389 there came up for probate the estate of Dikaiogenes, the rich but apparently unpedigreed man whose family alliance with the Gephyraioi has already been mentioned. Besides this influential connection, one of his greatgranddaughters married, first, the son of the demagogue Kleon and, second, the son of Lysias' attractive young client Mantitheos. Her sister's husband was brother-in-law to the great general Chabrias. The family tree includes generals, cavalry commanders, treasurers, a secretary to the Council, and at least six trierarchs; these rich bourgeois show a record of public service worthy of the old aristocracy, and unmatched by any other clients of the probatelawyer Isaios, through whom we know these details.[34]

Lysias' Funeral Oration and Plato's *Menexenos*

Young Mantitheos had served, like Kallias, in the Corinthian war (395–386). We possess from the pen of the resident alien Lysias a funeral oration over the dead in the war.[35] It is interesting to compare and contrast this oration

with Perikles' speech and with others of this century:
Plato's in the *Menexenos,* which is a parody, of the same
dramatic date as Lysias' (Plato himself may have fought
in the Corinthian War); [36] the one attributed to Demosthenes after Chaironeia (338); [37] and Hypereides' after
the Lamian War (322).[38] Perikles' famous oration was
profoundly aristocratic in tone. The same cannot be said
of Lysias'. The conventional catch phrases are there:
bravery, noble death, fighting for freedom, victory, triumph
over Fate, the glory of the ancestors. But there is an under-
lying negative tone, an evidence of a failure of nerve, which
is completely typical of the unaristocratic fourth century.
The word of highest frequency is *kindynos,* "risk, danger."
It is true that the risks are said to be run voluntarily by
brave men fighting for freedom, but the timidity is un-
mistakable, there is a compulsive emphasis on death and
misfortune, and the author, himself unpedigreed and not a
citizen, refers much less often to ancestors than does an
aristocrat like Perikles or Plato.

Plato's attempt ironically expresses his detached aristocratic displeasure at chauvinism; he underlines this by putting the speech into the mouth of Perikles' mistress Aspasia.
Because it is a parody of the high rhetorical style,[39] the
word of highest frequency is *kosmein,* "to set in beautiful
order." The ancestors are there, the glory, the fight for
freedom, the *polis.* Perhaps there is a trace of the genuine
pride of this descendant of kings in the praise of the
Athenians as the only truebred, autochthonous Hellenes.[40]

The Aristocracy 384–354

The Attic civil year 384/3 was a fateful one for history:
in it were born Philip of Macedon, who was to bring Athens
to her knees; Demosthenes, who tried to save her; and
Aristotle of Stageira, who left her in time of crisis "lest
she should sin a second time against philosophy." At the
time of their birth a significant figure, Plato's only rival

on the Athenian intellectual scene, was the rhetorician and pamphleteer Isokrates, whose school, attended by princes, was a rival to Plato's Academy. The names of forty-one of his pupils are known: they include Nikokles king of Cyprus, the orators Isaios and Hypereides, the general Timotheos, and the historians Androtion, Ephoros, Theopompos, and perhaps Xenophon. It is perhaps significant that only Timotheos and Androtion have possible gentile affiliations; did the gennetai favor Plato's Academy? Isokrates himself belonged to the bourgeoisie, though he tried to place upon his ideas an aristocratic stamp; [41] that is, he advocated a return to the "ancestral constitution" based on a property qualification, and, on the basis of the harmony thus achieved, a Panhellenic crusade against Persia, whose king had become virtual overlord of the Ionian Greeks under a peace signed in 386. Isokrates expressed these views for the first time in his *Panegyrikos,* written for the Olympic games of 380, in which he mentions incidentally that at the Mysteries the Eumolpids and the Kerykes solemnly pronounce an interdict against the Persians and other barbarians.[42]

By 378/7 fear either of Persians or of Spartans was sufficiently remote that the Athenians were emboldened to set up a Second Naval Confederacy, profiting from the mistakes of the first. We have the charter of the confederacy, inscribed on stone: [43] for our purposes the significant thing is that the old aristocracy apparently took no initiative in this important undertaking; neither the mover of the decree, Aristotle of Marathon, nor the Aristeides of the new league, Kallistratos of Aphidna, is from a known genos. The only evidence of aristocratic involvement is an alliance of the previous year with Thebes.[44] Its mover, Stephanos, perhaps son of Antidorides of Eroiadai, is recorded as *kalos kai agathos,*[45] his clan unmentioned. Relations with a foreign power were cemented (375 or 373) by a decree in honor of the king of Sidon. Its mover was named Menexenos,[46] a name which occurs in the family tree of Dikaiogenes as given in Isaios' oration on his estate: since a Menexenos is also the mover of the previously mentioned Demotionidai decree, the family may belong to this clan,[47] but without patronymics or demotics the identification is hazardous.

In 373 the ungrateful Athenians removed from the generalship one of the few major figures of his time who may have been a gennetes. This was Timotheos son of Konon of the deme Anaphlystos, in the silver-mining region of Attica.[48] In two very late inscriptions in Eleusis,[49] women from the family of a *daidouchos* (torchbearer), a post hereditary in the genos of Kerykes, boast descent from Konon. This is the evidence for assuming that Konon, the famous victor over the Spartans in the battle of Knidos (394), and his son Timotheos were Kerykes.[50] Timotheos was a friend of Plato and, as we saw, a pupil of Isokrates. At his father's death (about 389), Timotheos inherited seventeen talents—a considerable fortune—which he unselfishly expended in the support of military and naval operations. These gained for the new confederacy many allies, and for himself the honor of statues in the Agora and on the Akropolis. But his natural hauteur and, as Isokrates (who doted on him) says,[51] his inability to lower himself to the level of those intolerant of their natural superiors made him many enemies, who contrived to depose him from his generalship. He then entered the service of the Great King (373–368), but returned to Athens in 367, became reconciled with the rival general Iphikrates, and married his daughter to Iphikrates' son (362). Subsequently Timotheos fell victim to aristocratic feud: at an unknown date an Aristogeiton, perhaps a Gephyraios, made a speech against him, and in 354 he was accused of treason by the demagogue Aristophon (who may have been a Bouzyges).[52] He was fined the enormous sum of 100 talents, which even his great wealth was inadequate to pay, and retired brokenhearted to Chalkis in Euboia, where he died. The Athenians, repenting, allowed his son Konon to pay off the fine for ten talents,[53] and buried Timotheos in

a place of honor on the road to the Academy, where centuries later Pausanias saw his tomb.

If Timotheos' friend Plato was writing his *Republic* at
fifty-five, the age at which he says man reaches the height
of his mental development, then it appeared about 372.
Although this is not the place for full treatment, it should
at least be said that the Philosopher-King is the Athenian
aristocrat idealized and intellectualized. The guardian or
silver class sounds like the military aristocracy (generals
father and son) mentioned above, as does the timocratic
man with his distrust of ideas, his devotion to hunting, his
contentiousness and self-will.[54] It is interesting, in view
of J. V. A. Fine's hypothesis that alienation of land is a
cause of the decline of the aristocracy, to notice that for
Plato the decline from the timocratic to the oligarchic state
begins when citizens are first allowed to mortgage and sell
their patrimony.[55] In describing the oligarchic man's greed
of gain, Plato reveals the born aristocrat's scorn of money
made in trade. But his deepest loathing is reserved for the
radical democracy that killed his beloved Sokrates,[56] with
its licentious and unqualified demagogues, its flouting of
the aristocratic virtues of reverence and moderation—a
passage reminiscent of that other aristocrat, Thoukydides,
describing the perversion of values on Kerkyra two generations before.

Plato records the hospitality of the Keryx Kallias, son
of Hipponikos, to visiting philosophers. Kallias was, as
we know, a peace commissioner to Sparta in 371; one of
his colleagues was the demagogue Aristophon's son Demostratos, who bears the name of his grandfather, the Bouzyges of the time of Perikles.[57] Less than three weeks after
the treaty was signed, Thebes won the battle of Leuktra,
and the period of Spartan supremacy was over.

Though the short-lived Theban hegemony (371–362)
was unpopular among laconizing Athenian aristocrats,
there is no evidence that it harmed the Athenian economy.
On the contrary, a group of forty-five records of Laureion

silver-mine leases, dating from about 367/6, which were found in the Agora,[58] bear the names of many of the nouveaux riches who profited from these mines, and of a few aristocrats. Among aristocrats of unspecified genos are Nikias' grandson, one Lysitheides,[59] referred to elsewhere by the aristocratic epithet *kalos kai agathos* (rich, a pupil of Isokrates, and rewarded for services to the city with a golden crown); and Mantias and Mantitheos,[60] son and grandson of Lysias' young client. Of attested gennetai, the leases mention the politician Polyeuktos,[61] son of Sostratos of Spettos, an Amynandrid (more about him later); and Diokles of Sounion,[62] who belonged to Alkibiades' possible genos, the Salaminioi.

An inscription of 363/2 has cast a flood of new light on the Salaminioi.[63] The stone records the settlement by arbitration of a dispute over religious prerogatives between two branches of the genos. The priesthoods involved are those of Athena Skiras, Herakles at the ferry, Eurysakes, Aglauros—in whose shrine the ephebes (cadets) took their oath—Pandrosos and Kourotrophos. Diokles, the mine-lessee, is related to Diphilos, the archon of the Sounion branch, and a number of other significant names are recorded, including treasurers of Athena, Areopagites, councilors, mineowners, and contributors. One of them, Hegias son of Hegesias of Sounion, was the brother of Hegesandros and Hegesippos,[64] two statesmen of the second rank who will be discussed further below. Three points about the genos are worth noting: first, in supplying the priestess of Athena Skiras,[65] it was involved with the Theseus myth (and Theseus was heroized in this century by conservative partisans of the ancestral constitution), because Theseus was believed to have sailed for Krete from Phaleron, where the temple was. The temple was visited during the vintage festival of the Oschophoria by two handsome young men— one from each branch of the genos—with vine leaves in their hair and wearing the old Ionic chiton to symbolize the dress of the maiden victims who sailed with Theseus for

Krete. But, second, with a name like Salaminioi, the genos
can hardly be as old as Mycenaean Athens, nor can it ante-
date the struggle between Athens and Megara for Salamis
in the seventh century; it will have come into being to
promote and justify the claim of Athens to the island. Thus
at two stages the history of the clan shows mythology
serving as a tool of politics. Third, the clan as a corporation
owned land—an archaic feature—from the income of which
its sacrifices were financed.

A cult-calendar of this period (375–350), from the deme
Erchia, has been interpreted as indicating cult-transfer
from gentile to nongentile hands: the main aim is alleged
to be to get the sacrifices paid for, no matter by whom;
and the careful specifying of the locale of the various
sacrifices is taken to suggest either that they had been
moved from their traditional locus, or that the participants
were no longer expected to have a clansman's knowledge
of such details.[66]

Hegesandros and Hegesippos, the two politically active
brothers of Hegias of the Salaminian genos, were both ar-
dent democrats, to the point of chauvinism.[67] This meant
that they did not advocate peace at any price; they favored
the use of force, if necessary, to preserve democratic
regimes among Athen's allies, and in 357/6 each sponsored
decrees to this effect,[68] which have been preserved on stone.
Hegesandros,[69] the younger brother, in true aristocratic
fashion married an heiress and, according to his right-wing
enemies, was involved in escapades of truly Alkibidean
amorality, of which the least unsavory involved gambling,
brawling, and cock-fighting. Lawsuits resulted; his fellow
clansman Diopeithes of Sounion, chosen arbitrator, contrived to save Hegesandros from the consequences of his
acts. Just so members of the *hetaireiai* had helped each
other in Alkibiades' day. Hegesandros was paymaster to
a general—lining his pockets to Athens' cost, his enemies
said—and treasurer of Athena (361/0). Hegesippos was as
picturesque as his younger brother; he was known as

Krobylos (Topknot), from his old-fashioned, aristocratic way of wearing his hair. He was an orator; a speech of his is extant, which will be discussed in its proper place below. In 359 Philip II had come to the throne of Macedon; Hegesippos saw him as a menace and remained his uncompromising enemy to the end. In 356 Philip's son Alexander was born, whose world-shaking exploits were to stand in such sharp contrast to the sophomoric antics alleged against aristocratic young Athenians like Hegesandros.

One of the colleagues of the brothers from Sounion in democratic politics was Polyeuktos son of Sostratos of Sphettos,[70] whom we find proposing honors in 356/5 to the ambassadors of a Thracian town loyal to the Athenian demos. He was immensely fat, and when heated with oratory puffed and sweated in a ludicrous way.[71] Since a Sostratos of Sphettos appears in a late list of clansmen of the Amynandridai,[72] it is a plausible assumption that the fourth-century Polyeuktos belonged to this clan. It supplied the priest of Kekrops, mythical King of Athens, worshiped on the Akropolis in a shrine adjoining the Erechtheum. We shall meet Polyeuktos again. In a long career he never faltered in his hostility to Macedon. After the disaster at Chaironeia he was high on Alexander's list of wanted Athenians.

It is the conservative bourgeois opposition, not the old-line aristocracy, whose point of view Isokrates states in his *Areopagitikos* (355).[73] He has no use for aristocrats like Perikles, who were champions of the people: "When we imagined that our power was invincible, we barely escaped being enslaved" (6), and he holds Perikles' generation ultimately responsible for present day degeneracy (50), "when men are sprung from noble ancestors and yet are only a little better than those who are distinguished for depravity." (72) When he speaks of the present neglect of the old religion (29–30), we may take this as evidence for the decline of the gene, because the examples to the contrary collected in this chapter are, it must be emphasized, the exception, not the rule. The tasteless extravagance of new rites, which he also mentions, is the work of parvenus, not the gene. The paternalism of the old gene, setting up their clients on rented farms, as commercial travelers, or in small businesses was a fact in the sixth century (32), but, as Isokrates exploits it, it is "an idealized dressing up of the naked economic interests of the propertied classes." [74] The Areiopagos which he would set up as a censor of morals now consisted, not of the old pedigreed aristocracy—with all their imperfections on their heads— but of the nouveaux riches. Unlike Perikles or Plato, Isokrates in his calculus of values put the intellectual life last (45), listing as suitable leisure-class occupations "riding horseback, athletics, hunting with dogs, and philosophy." Even if he intends the order to be climactic, the juxtaposition in ludicrous. What he would return to, the old democracy of Solon and Kleisthenes, is in fact an old-fashioned laissez-faire oligarchy, in which the people would be taught to work and save, and mind their own business— not to live out of the public trough, but to leave public administration to those who could afford it (24–26).

The Aristocracy 354–341

Isokrates was not active in politics, except indirectly through his pamphlets. The leader of the conservatives between 354 and 350 was the financier Euboulos, a non-interventionist who saw as his chief duty the caretakership of the material interests of the bourgeoisie to which he belonged.[75] In his zeal to increase public revenues in all possible ways, he tried (*ca.* 350/49) to rent out a tract of sacred land on the border between Attika and Megara, but the Eumolpids and Kerykes, led by the hierophant Lakrateides and the daidouchos Hierokleides, using the combined prestige of their clan and of the Delphic oracle, circumvented him.[76] Demosthenes, the fieriest patriot of this century, started out in Euboulos' faction, and while in it gave some good, cautious Periklean advice against rashness,[77] but he soon grew impatient of isolationism and broke with the noninterventionists.

Neither bourgeois oligarchs, nor radical democrats, nor old-line aristocrats were happy in these years. 353 is the dramatic date of the *Seventh Epistle* attributed to Plato. It purports to describe his state of mind a generation earlier, but it breathes the world-weariness of a man of seventy who has never found reason for faith in any existing constitution. His ambitions for a political career had turned to disgust as the conduct of his own class in the oligarchical revolutions of the 400 and the Thirty, "and the judicial murder of Socrates by the restored democracy ripened the conviction that all existing governments were irremediably corrupt and that nothing less than a miracle would redeem them."[78] His abortive attempt to set up a philosopher-king in Sicily, and his assessment of the Athenian scene since his return in 360 had done nothing to make his view less jaundiced. Not Plato but Demosthenes was fated to make the brave but ill-starred effort to make the Athenians react faster to the shadows in the Cave.

Just before his death, in 347, Plato published his immensely long and disenchanted *Laws*, the fruit of an intelligent aristocrat's disillusion. The book has a well-deserved reputation for being reactionary, with its plea for censorship, its deprecation of change, its peculiarly academic punishment for atheists (they have to listen to lectures [908 A], and those who fail will be liquidated), and its sinister secret police, the Nocturnal Council. But there are two other noteworthy points about the *Laws* that are not so often made. One is that it is an aristocrat's book: it emphasizes *aidôs* (647 A 10), that supreme virtue of aristocratic youth which Shorey has brilliantly translated "fear of the Lord."[79] It puts forth (along with other qualifications like seniority and wisdom) the claim of birth to

rule (690 A). It sets up a polity which shall be a mean
between monarchy and democracy (756 E) : that mean is
aristocracy. The other point is that it is written with a
clear idea—perhaps traditional in Plato's family—of
archaic Athens: the "wardens of the law" (753 A) are
the old Areiopagites; the legendary Dodekapolis of early
Athens is mentioned (848 C), and in the detailed provi-
sions for the distribution of property (923 A–926 A) gentile principles are at work. The *Laws* is undeniably a
morose and overly didactic book, but the aristocratic ethic
and the sense of history that pervade it take some of the
curse off its hyperconservatism, and against this criticism
it is possible to argue that there are "all-pervading corre-
spondences in principle and in detail" with the *Republic*.[80]

In 346 a ten-year war between Athens and Philip over
Amphipolis was settled, to Philip's advantage, by the
Peace of Philokrates. We are fortunate enough to possess
three documents from the years 346–342, two of them by
gennetai, bearing on relations with Philip. The first, Isokrates' *Philippos,* represents the point of view not of the
aristocracy, either radical or conservative, but of the rich
bourgeoisie. It is an invitation to Philip to unite the Greeks
in a war against Persia. Analysis of word-frequencies shows
it to be a protreptic—Panhellenic, patriotic, aggressive,
practical, antibarbarian, conscious of the role of force and
of Fortune, rhetorical, yet pessimistic, and escapist.[81] (Con-
sistency was not one of Isokrates' strong points.) From the
point of view of an Athenian patriot like Demosthenes or
Hegesippos, this is the appeal of a quisling. With hindsight,
we can see that Isokrates anticipated the success of Alexander. But by that time Athenian political autonomy was a
thing of the past.

The second document is Hegesippos' speech *On Halon-
nesos* (343/2), a North-Aegean island which Philip held
and Athens claimed. Word-analysis shows that Hegesippos
was a man with a strong interest in the democratic process,

conventional and conservative in his aristocratic strong sense of property, legal-minded but flexible, eager to appeal to the consensus of mankind as to the justice of Athens' case.[82] He is angry at the influence of Philip's creatures in Athens, and touchy about Athens' not losing face. On an embassy to Philip in 343 about Halonnesus and other matters, his conduct is reported as undiplomatic.

The third document is a letter to Philip, of the same year, from Speusippos son of Eurymedon of Myrrhinous, Plato's nephew and successor as head of the Academy.[83] Speusippos, seeing Isokrates as a rival for Philip's favor, tells the King that Isokrates has not said enough about Philip's benefactions or about his claims to recognition as a Hellene with territorial rights in Greece, because of his descent from Herakles. Here again mythology is being used in political propaganda; Speusippos may have had access to some traditions about the Late Bronze and Early Iron Age handed down in his genos, the Medontidai. The use of these traditions as flattering arguments to a Macedonian monarch against Athens' interests leaves an unpleasant taste in the mouths of those who admire Demosthenes' stand for Athenian freedom. For our purposes the significant thing is to see the diametrically opposed stands of two members of the aristocracy: Hegesippos the champion of the people in the Periklean tradition; Speusippos the cosmopolitan in the fashion of Perikles' enemies. To Athens as an ideal, Speusippos feels no more loyalty than did the Old Oligarch, whose small-mindedness he shares.

The democratic, anti-Macedonian faction was not idle in the face of this pamphleteering. In 343 Demosthenes, Polyeuktos, and Hegesippos went on a successful embassy through the Peloponnese, lining up allies for Athens. If Demosthenes was a Bouzyges, we have here an embassy consisting entirely of gennetai, and all three in the Periklean tradition.

On the other hand, not all gennetai were politically active or economically prosperous. A speech of 343 [84] names

seven gennetai from a clan, the Brytidai, which is so
obscure that we do not know what cult it served (the root
seems to have something to do with wine lees). Yet three
of its named members are recorded elsewhere as playing
a part in the public life of their time. Eualkos (Eualkes in
the manuscripts) of Phaleron was president of the Boule
in 322/1,[85] Euphranor son of Sokratides of Aigilia served
as an arbitrator about mid-century,[86] and Nikippos of
Kephale contributed to a religious dedication about 324,
and helped to equip a trireme about 323/2.[87]

The Brytidai, then, contributed in their modest way to
the war effort. Athens had need of all the contributions
she could get, for opinion within the city was far from
united: Philip's partisans were obstructive, expressing, for
example, righteous indignation when Philip complained
of the invasion of his sphere of influence by the Salaminian
Diopeithes of Sounion. Demosthenes defended the clansman with spirit in *On the Chersonese* (341).[88] Diopeithes'
appeal for reinforcements evoked in support, shortly thereafter, one of Demosthenes' masterpieces, the *Third Philip-
pic*,[89] arguing the need for action in the face of Philip's
imperialistic drive, which had tripled the extent of his
kingdom since his accession. Demosthenes is said to have
known Thoukydides by heart, and to have reproduced him
from memory when fire destroyed his library. This speech
is full of Thoukydidean echoes: the diagnosis of disease in
the body politic, the emphasis on foresight (which is
Thoukydides' touchstone for distinguishing a statesman
like Perikles from a mere politician), and on Athens as
the school of Greece (73). He appeals, in the aristocratic
way, to the ancestral tradition, with more than hackneyed
rhetoric, for he combines the appeal with a pragmatic
exposition of disagreeable facts, and proposals of practical
solutions: collect funds, send ships, make alliances, "sum-
mon, collect, instruct, and exhort the rest of the Greeks."
One hears more than an echo of Perikles.

Chaironeia and After

Demosthenes' superhuman attempt to galvanize his fellow Athenians to a laborious outlay of civic virtue finally bore fruit, but it was too little and too late: when Philip swooped down upon Greece, the Athenians and their allies met him at Chaironeia (338), but they were defeated, and the defeat marked the end of Athenian political autonomy. Philip danced a drunken dance upon the field of victory, mockingly repeating the name, patronymic, and demotic of Demosthenes. The orator was chosen to deliver the funeral oration over the fallen. The speech that has come down to us under his name may well be his: [90] it is steeped in Thoukydidean reminiscence, and it emphasizes as no other extant funeral speech does the claims of the gene to Athenian gratitude. At the same time, to avoid offending the unpedigreed, this good democrat calls the roll of the ten Attic tribes: they, too, have patronymic names, and their members died worthily of a great tradition.

Defeat did not daunt the spirit of the anti-Macedonian faction, and Philip was disposed to be lenient. His partisan Isokrates died soon after the battle, though it did not "kill with report that old man eloquent." Among Philip's foes, Hegesippos courageously proposed honors for loyal Athenian allies,[91] and a group of Athenians, including a descendant of Themistokles, paid for an inscription awarding a crown to the demos.[92] (Another possible descendant of Themistokles appears in a list of councilors dated 336/5).[93] In 336 the demos passed a decree granting immunity to the slayer of anyone proposing to set up a tyranny:[94] what they feared was the pro-Macedonian faction in the plutocratic Areiopagos. Shortly after the passage of this decree Philip was murdered, and the Athenians passed a decree praising the murderers. Philip's son and successor Alexander, incensed at this, demanded that the Athenians yield up to him five generals and five orators, among the latter Demosthenes, Lykourgos, and Polyeuktos. The Athenians did not comply: the next year we find Polyeuktos opposing honors for the pro-Macedonian orator Demades. On the other hand, despite the failure of his policy at Chaironeia, the Athenians proposed (336) a golden crown for Demosthenes. His enemies attacked the proposal as illegal, and the crown was not then awarded. Litigation on the matter was delayed for six years: Demosthenes' speech in defense of his policy (330) is his unquestioned masterpiece.

Lykourgos the Eteoboutad

The core of Athenian resistance between 336 and 324 was the old-fashioned, blue-blooded, puritanical orator and financial genius, the Eteoboutad Lykourgos, son of Lykophron of Boutadai. He approaches three-dimensionality for us through an ancient *Life*,[95] a number of inscriptions, and a speech. His family had deserved well of the democracy: his grandfather had been executed by the Thirty. He studied with Plato and Isokrates, but retained "an innate outspokenness because of his good birth." He did not share Isokrates' fondness for monarchy, and mocked at the deification of Alexander the Great, inquiring, "What sort of god is it when those who *come out* of his temple have to sprinkle themselves with holy water?"[96] He increased the city's revenue twentyfold, to 1200 talents a year—no mean feat in the lean times after Chaironeia—and in his three four-year terms as financial administrator distributed 18,900 talents. Much of the money he used to restore the fleet,[97] but he was also a builder in the aristocratic tradition:[98] Athens owed to him an arsenal, an enlargement of the theater of Dionysos, a Panathenaic stadium, the Lykeion where Aristotle taught, and the embellishment of the Pnyx,[99] seat of the ekklesia, core of the democracy.

In Lykourgos, puritan austerity emerges most sharply. In his concentration on public business, he was a man for

all seasons. He was as famed for justice as Aristeides, but
not for mercy: he signed warrants against evil-doers with
a pen dipped not in ink but in death, as his vindictive
speech *Against Leokrates* (330) shows. Leokrates had fled
Athens after Chaironeia. Lykourgos calls him traitor: he
uses the word for treason and its congeners seventy-two
times in the speech. The reverse of the coin, patriotism, is
the second leitmotif: *patris* (fatherland) occurs sixty-one
times. But the patriotism is savage to the point of sadism:
the evidence is the frequency of the words for death, punishment, vengeance, hatred. Yet Lykourgos had heeded
Perikles' adjuration to become a lover of Athens: his per-
oration appeals to his fellow citizens in the name of the
country and its trees (the sacred olive of Athena whose
priestess his clan provided), the harbors, dockyards, walls,
temples, and sanctuaries which he had built, restored, or
embellished. The page-long quotations from poets,[100] the
historical and mythological digressions were not irrelevant
to a man who had the traditions of his city in the marrow
of his bones.

Lykourgos' puritanism is revealed also by his prohibition
against riding in carriages to Eleusis and the simplicity of
his dress and habits: he usually went unshod and wore the
same cloak winter and summer; he rehearsed his speeches
night and day, deliberately sleeping on an uncomfortable
cot to encourage insomnia. Even when he lay at death's
door, he had himself carried to the Council House to render
the account of his stewardship required by law.

He had the aristocrats' antiquarian interest in the
glorious past: he commissioned authorized texts of the
tragic poets,[101] revived old cults,[102] and encouraged new,
for as an old-fashioned gennetes he was deeply religious.
Commemorative paintings of the history of his clan, with
likenesses of all the priests of Poseidon Erechtheus, were
on display in the Erechtheum.[103] He died in 324 and was
buried at public expense in the place of honor on the
Academy road.

For a time after his death Athens, as the creature of Macedon under Demetrios of Phaleron, was in no position to do him honor, but in 307/6 twelve distinguished citizens of the revived democracy decreed him crowns;[104] the demos decreed also a bronze statue; and maintenance in the Prytaneion for the eldest son of his line in perpetuity.[105] Descendants intermarried with the Eumolpids and Kerykes and kept the priestly tradition alive. About 330, the Kerykes honored one Xenokles son of Xeiris of Sphettos, applying to him the same title assigned by the literary sources to Lykourgos. He will have been one of the friends in whose name Lykourgos was elected to a second or third term in order to evade the prohibition against iteration in office. Xenokles was superintendent of the mysteries in 321/0 and in this capacity built a bridge on the Sacred Way. Could this bridgebuilder have been a Gephyraios? In any case he was closely associated with Kerykes: in 338/7 he shared with the Keryx Konon, son of the general, the cost of a trireme.[106]

Local History

Lykourgos' antiquarian interests were part of the atmosphere of that age, in which it must have seemed to many that Athens' future was likely to be less glorious than her past. The Aristotelian *Constitution of Athens,* that primer of constitutional history and citizens' handbook, reflecting the piety of the times,[107] was written in this tradition; so too the antiquarian local history of the so-called Atthidographers who flourished after 350. Four concern us: Kleidemos, Androtion, Phanodemos, and Philochoros.[108] Kleidemos was not a gennetes, but was related by marriage to Philochoros, who was probably a Keryx.[109] Androtion's genos is not known, but he came from a distinguished and wealthy family, studied under Isokrates, and was the only Atthidographer who was also active in politics, where he acquired a reputation for moderation and honesty.[110] Phanodemos was more democratic than the rest; a supporter of Lykourgos, he served with him, and with Nikias' great-grandson Nikeratos, on religious boards at Oropos (329/8) and Delphi (*ca.* 330) [111] which have been described as a cross-section of the ruling class in Athens of that time; [112] in a list of contributors of 328/7 he appears with Polyeuktos and a Philaid, Oulias, descended from Miltiades and Kimon.[113] (A Miltiades kept up the age-old family tradition by founding a colony in the Adriatic about 325/4.[114]) Philochoros, the most important of the four—we have more of his fragments than of the other three combined—properly belongs to the next generation, but may conveniently be mentioned here. His father Kyknos was honored by his fellow councilors in 334/3.[115] The son is revealed by the fragments as a true scholar and a "religious conservative." [116] All but Phanodemos set a tone for the times, of quietism, implying the hope that if Athens can "minister to the values of culture and religion" it can preserve itself as "an island of peace in the struggle of the great powers." [117]

Reorganization of Ephebes

A combination of this spirit and the greater belligerence of Lykourgos is to be seen in the reorganization at this time of the ephebes, a cadet corps of young men eighteen to twenty, who, under their *sophronistes* (moderator) and *kosmetes* (orderer) not only made a pious pilgrimage to the sanctuaries, but also formed a home guard at the Peiraieus and at the border forts. Plato had advocated such a corps in the *Laws*.[118]

Last Years (330–322)

Lykourgos may have been able to interpose delays in the suit on the illegality of the proposal to crown Demosthenes, which, as we know, had hung fire for six years. Demos-

thenes' opponent, Aischines,[119] may have been glad of the
delay in the days when Alexander's demand for the surrender of Demosthenes brought the orator's popularity to
unprecedented heights. But in 330, when Alexander's suc-
cesses in the East brought him to the summit of his glory,[120]
Aischines finally succeeded in bringing the case to trial.
Demosthenes' speech is an eloquent defense of his policy
of warning, vigilance, and action:[121] the key words are
prattein (to act) and *politeuesthai* (to carry out a policy).
His appeal to the *progonoi* is uniquely moving: Demosthenes
demanded that Athens live up to her traditions. ''It cannot
be, it cannot be that you were wrong, men of Athens, to
accept the risks of war for universal freedom and redemp-
tion; I swear it by our forefathers who bore the brunt of
battle at Marathon, who stood in warlike array at Plataia,
who fought the sea fights of Salamis and Artemision, and
by the many others who lie in the public tombs, brave men
all, buried there by a city that held them worthy of honor—
all, Aischines, not only the successful and victorious.''[122]
Demosthenes won his crown, and posterity has almost uni-
versally agreed with the verdict; Aischines did not even
get the minimum number of votes required to save him
from exile.

Grote called the speech *On the Crown* ''the funeral oration of extinct Athenian and Grecian freedom.''[123] But
that freedom still had another eight years. Soon thereafter,
Demosthenes was imprisoned for accepting bribes; he
escaped. In 323 Alexander died, and Athens, despite the
threat of famine,[124] revolted from Macedonia in the so-
called Lamian War.

Polyeuktos last appears in history as an ambassador,
who, with the help of the exiled Demosthenes, attempted
to detach Arkadia from allegiance to Macedon.[125] The
revolt was ill-starred and short-lived; Athens was defeated
at the battle of Krannon, and Demosthenes' one-time partisan Hypereides—not, so far as we know, a gennetes—
was chosen (322) to deliver the last funeral oration of
Greek freedom. Hypereides conceives the defeated general

as welcomed in Hades by the heroes of old, among them Miltiades and Themistokles, Harmodios and Aristogeiton, men of pedigree who all had struck a blow for freedom. The speech stays within the prescribed conventions, but with grace and imagination worthy of the last struggle for Hellenic liberty.[126] Demosthenes, who had taken refuge in the sanctuary of Poseidon at Kalauria, took poison concealed in a pen to escape falling into the hands of the Macedonians. With his death a great tradition faded, and Athens lapsed into the doldrums of the Hellenistic Age.

Two

The Gene in the Hellenistic Age (322–166)

Politically, Athens never again mattered in antiquity after the death of Demosthenes. Culturally, she continued to be a Mecca, and to her cultural prestige the gene contributed not a little. Furthermore the aristocratic clans continued to play a more or less honorable part in local politics, while in priesthoods and in festivals their prominence continued unabated.

After Demosthenes' death the Macedonian regent Antipater reduced the Athenian navy to impotence, and the city surrendered unconditionally, accepting a Macedonian garrison in the Peiraieus. The propertied pro-Macedonian faction took control, and the constitution was remodelled in an antidemocratic spirit, with a property qualification, suspension of support for the poor, and a return to what the ruling class was pleased to call "the Solonian constitution," based on the principle, which was not new, that "the leisure, independence, and self-interest which the ownership of property entailed, and the intelligence which a superior education promoted, gave the upper class a right both to determine the general policy, and to attend to the administration." [1]

It will be convenient, following Ferguson, to break the five generations with which this chapter is concerned into seven periods. The first (322–318) saw an abortive struggle for independence; the second (317–307) the aristocratic regime of Demetrios of Phaleron. The third (307–294) brought a restoration of moderate democracy: the dominant figure was Stratokles of Diomeia, not, as far as we know, a member of a genos; gennetai include Lykourgos' son Habron, Demosthenes' nephew Demochares (possible), and the philosopher Epikouros. In the fourth period (294–263) Athens was crushed between Macedon and Egypt; with the loss of the Chremonidean War (263), named for a gennetes, Athens became a Macedonian puppet (fifth period: 263–229), but during this difficult time (from 247/6) there began the rise to prominence of the aristocratic brothers Eurykleides and Mikion of Kephisia, under whom (229–198/7: sixth period) Athens successfully pur-

sued a policy of neutrality. With their deaths began the
seventh and final period (197/6–166), called by Ferguson
the age of the "Tory democracy," still dominated by the
family of Eurykleides and Mikion and their circle; by its
end, marked by the Romans' assignment to Athens of the
island of Delos, Athens began to pass forever into the orbit
of Rome.

The Abortive Struggle for Independence: 322–318

In the years of the abortive struggle for independence
the wealthy and the gennetai were not inactive. A list of
men who discharged liturgies (*IG* II², 417, after 330) is
headed *"Eutaxia"* (good order) an aristocratic catch-
word; one of those listed, Theopompos son of Pyrrhinos
of Gargettos, belonged to a family (genos unspecified) who
might well be described as among the elite of Hellenistic
Athens; its members continued to make donations to the
state down into the second century.² Between 330 and 320
the chief Eumolpid, the hierophant, appointed ten men to
make a lectisternium to Plouton (*IG* II², 1933); its members included dischargers of liturgies, members of the
Boule (who tend under a limited franchise to be distinguished persons), donors, and military men. One of them,
Eteokles son of Chremonides of Aithalidai, the father of
the general who lost the Chremonidean War, belonged to
the genos Praxiergidai, because his daughter was priestess
of Aglauros, an office hereditary in their clan. His statue
was set up some time in this period in the theater of
Dionysos.³ In 321/0 the Eleusis garrison honored Xenokles
the son of Xeinis of Sphettos, superintendent of the mysteries, builder of a bridge on the sacred way; the fact that
he had been honored earlier by the Kerykes (334/29) implies that he was himself a member of the genos. He was
sufficiently in favor with Macedon to elicit years later
(306/5) a gift of money from Antigonos.⁴

Among the philosophic schools the Lykeion, which, after
all, had been founded by the tutor of Alexander the Great,

was a center of pro-Macedonian feeling. Aristotle's successor Theophrastos has left us in his *Characters* a series of lifelike vignettes of the Athens of about 319.[5] Theophrastos is particularly malicious at the expense of anti-Macedonian aristocrats: his Boaster (*Char.* 23) brags that he is not too friendly with Macedon, and then preens himself on the five talents he has donated to relieve famine, on his trierarchies and other liturgies, his horse rearing and his family mansion which intends to sell because it is too small. But Theophrastos is not blind to the defects of his own faction: his Oligarch (*Char.* 26) thinks the ideal committee a committee of one, scorns the rabble (''it's Them or Us''), is a dandy and a snob, sneers at the mob's enslavement to the dole and the bribe, complains of the ruinousness of liturgies, and hates Theseus, who by this time had been propagandized into the most democratic of monarchs. His Man of Petty Ambition (21), proud of his status as a horseman, goes clanking about the agora in his spurs. The Evil Speaker (28) condemns in a breath all that Perikles and Demosthenes stood for: freedom of speech, democracy, autonomy. Reaction and piety go hand in hand, and the Eleusinian clans profit: one man (*Char.* 3) has set up an excessively large torch at the Mysteries (the office of daidouchos or torchbearer was, as shown above, hereditary among the Kerykes); another (16) runs to the Eumolpid expounder of canon law for an interpretation if a mouse has gnawed through his meal bag.

The Regime of Demetrios of Phaleron: 317–307

Out of the school of Theophrastos came Demetrios of Phaleron,[6] the man nominated in 317 by the Macedonian Kassandros as dictator of Athens. He belonged to the genos of Conon and Timotheus, who, as we know, were Kerykes. He was handsome and dandified, with his hair dyed blond. His reputation in antiquity, where conservatives generally controlled the means of propaganda, was higher than now; Cicero especially revered his memory as, like himself,

orator, theoretician, and practitioner of politics: "mirabi-
liter doctrinam ex umbraculis eruditorum otioque non
modo in solem atque in pulverem, sed in ipsum discrimen
aciemque producit" (*De Leg.* 3.14). Cicero wrote of him
elsewhere, again perhaps with himself in mind, "Doctus
vir Atheniensium rem publicam exsanguem iam et iacentem
sustentavit" (Rep. 2.1). Some ranked him with Drakon
and Solon, as the third lawgiver of Athens. He studied
oratory with Demosthenes' enemy Demarchos and philosophy with Theophrastos; his study of ethics did not dis-
suade him from arranging surrender terms which involved
the execution of his brother Himeraios, an anti-Macedonian;
on the other hand his philosophical interests led him to
secure the acquittal of Theodoros of Kyrene, the Atheist,
charged with impiety. His status as head of state was un-
constitutional: Polybios calls him *prostates* (champion—
but of whom?), a term once used of Perikles; Diodoros
equivocally names him *epimeletes* (superintendent), a
bureaucratic term widely used in fourth-century Athens.

Demetrios set up new magistrates called *nomophylakes*
(wardens of the law) and *gynaikonomoi* (regulators of
women—an unenviable post) whose job it was to enforce
new sumptuary laws designed to reduce extravagance, in
grave monuments (a mortal blow to Attic sculpture), in
banquets, and in women's dress. He ordered these econ-
omies though his own extravagance was proverbial—at least
among his enemies—and he did nothing to prevent the
erection of no fewer than 360 statues of himself. He increased the number of jurors in political trials to 1500,
bound, in a narrow franchise, to be members of the propertied class. To decrease the financial burden on his own
partisans, he abolished the obligation to pay for dramatic
choruses and placed the dramatic contests under the direc-
tion of a public official, the *agonothetes*—this probably in
the year of his archonship (309/8), an office to which he
had himself elected in order to pass into the Areiopagos,
whose aristocratic traditions would be useful to his regime.
Like a new Peisistratos, he entrusted the recitations of

Homer on state occasions to specialists. As a financier, he rivalled Lykourgos, bringing the annual revenues up to 1200 talents. He boasted of prosperity and low prices, and provided a pension for the descendants of Aristeides; however, no generalizations about his benevolence to the poor are warranted from this act, since the recipients were, as has not been noticed, Demetrios' fellow clansmen. Like earlier generations of gennetai who had been chiefs of state, Demetrios prided himself on horse rearing and chariot victories in the games; like them, too, he was repeatedly elected general. But his generalship did not prevent the loss of Lemnos, Imbros, and Delos, and his victories in dramatic contests show that the extravagance which he curbed in others he allowed for himself. Yet his personal excesses did not interfere with the efficiency of his administration. He conducted the first census recorded in Greek history: 21,000 citizens, 10,000 metics, perhaps 30,000 slaves; a total, including wives and children, of 200,000 to 250,000.

Demetrios' regime depended upon the Macedonian garrison, and when intrigue in Macedonia brought to power a faction committed to autonomy for Greek cities, his regime fell. Demetrios fled to Thebes and later to Alexandria, where he devoted himself to scholarly pursuits: writing on politics, on laws, and on his own administration; cooperating with Ptolemy I in collecting books for the Alexandrian Library. Falling out of favor with the second Ptolemy, he committed suicide (283), allowing himself, like Kleopatra later, to be bitten by an asp. The Athenians condemned him to death *in absentia* and tore down all but one of his statues. So ended the regime of which Plutarch wrote in conscious imitation of Thoukydides on Pericles, *Egeneto logoi men oligarchike ergoi de monarchike katastasis*, "There came into being what was in theory an oligarchy, in practice a monarchical constitution."

Though the Phalerean, unless Vitruvius is right in assigning Philo's portico at Eleusis to this time,[7] had not emulated the elaborate building program of earlier gennetai in power, he had been interested in maintaining

Athens as a place where literature might flourish. The
greatest poet of Athenian New Comedy, Menander, was his
friend and contemporary, and almost involved in his down-
fall.[8] It is from Menander's plays, as from Theophrastos'
Characters, that we can discern the flavor of *fin de siècle*
Athens. The recently discovered *Dyskolos,* written perhaps
early in Demetrios' regime, may, for example, contain in
the misanthrope's denunciation of extravagance in sacrifice
(447–453) a reflection of the Phalerean's sumptuary laws.[9]
Menander was the poet of the aristocrats (he won few first
prizes) and his picture of them, like Theophrastos', is not
always flattering, showing them as it does, bent upon ''common pleasure in youth and common gain in old age.'' [10]
Nonetheless this picture is a valuable corrective to any
mistaken notions we may have of every Athenian aristocrat
being as aloof and austere as Lykourgos. (The Phalerean
Demetrios himself, with his luxurious tastes, might be a
character out of Menander; he was only about thirty-three
when Kassandros brought him to power.) Menander shows
us, with only partial exaggeration, the members of the
jeunesse dorée sowing their wild oats, their fathers cheating
their wives; both groups consort with prostitutes and pan-
ders, frequent low dives, support parasites, are twisted
round the fingers of clever slaves. He makes real for us the
background against which were played out the lives of
men and women who otherwise would exist only as broken
names in an inscription, or incidental references of a historian more interested in the events on a wider stage.
Menander shows us the deep conservatism of the back-
country rustics like Demea in Terence's *Adelphoe* or
Knemon in the *Dyskolos,* the swagger of the mercenary
soldier, the purse-proud attitude of the rich men—in the
banks, or at the Peiraieus docks, or on their business trips
abroad—making the money which may admit their sons or
grandsons into the charmed circle of the aristocratic clans.

Moderate Democracy Restored

The liberator of Athens was another Demetrios, son of
Antigonos I of Macedonia, later ironically called Poliorketes
(Sacker-of-Cities), for his notorious failure in the siege of
Rhodes. He married, among others, a Philaid, Euthydike,[11]
descendant of Miltiades and Kimon, whose previous husband had been Ophelas, tyrant of Kyrene; dynastic marriages were still a source of power for the old gene. The
pious connections of his wife's clan did not deter Poliorketes from celebrating notorious orgies in the Parthenon
itself, temple of the maiden goddess.[12]

The key political figure of this period, Stratokles of
Diomeia,[13] was not, so far as we know, a gennetes, but he
found it politic to honor the memory of one, Lykourgos,[14]
and Lykourgos' son Habron won fame as Stratokles' asso-
ciate in rebuilding the Long Walls. He was in charge of
the general administration and the military funds, giving
up to his brother Lykophron, no doubt because of the
demands of this secular office, the priesthood of Poseidon
Erechtheus, which was hereditary in the Eteoboutad
genos.[15] Lykourgos' wife Kallisto was the daughter of
Habron of Bate, after whom their son was named. The
office of priestess of Athena Polias, hereditary in the
Eteoboutad genos, could descend through the female line:
a Lysistratos of Bate made a dedication to the priestess at
the end of the fourth century, and a daughter of Polyeuktos
of Bate served as priestess in 234/4.[16] Twelve citizens
joined Stratokles in proposing the posthumous honors for
Lykourgos: the names of ten of them are legible, inscribed
in crowns, on the stone (*IG* II², 3207). Of these, four were
Lykourgos' fellow tribesmen and one, Timodemos of
Acharnai, was a gennetes. Pindar is not very helpful when
he refers to one of his ancestors, Nemean victor, as belonging to the Timodemidai,[17] which may refer to a family, not
a genos. The family lived on Salamis; is the genos the
Salaminioi?

Not only Lykourgos' son, but Demosthenes' nephew, Demochares of Leukonoe, was prominent in politics in this generation. Demochares was the greater orator's sister's son and thus possibly a Bouzyges on his mother's side. He efficiently provided offensive and defensive weapons for the war of 307–304,[18] went into exile at the time of the short-lived change of government the next year, but returned in 286/5. An honorific decree of 271/0, moved by his son Laches, makes the proud claim that Demochares was never an oligarch. As a democrat, he joined in the persecution of that oligarchic stronghold, the Peripatetic school, hounding Theophrastos into exile with arguments of guilt by association. But fortunately for the future of Athens as the home of academic freedom, the prosecution lost and Theophrastos returned.[19]

Freedom of association being now guaranteed, Epikouros now (306, early summer) came from Lampsakos and set up his famous school in the Garden. He was a Philaid,[20] of the genos of Miltiades, a far cry from that sixth-century ancestor whose nickname was the Simpleton. Perhaps his practical assessment of the witch-hunting temper of the times operated as powerfully as his desire not to upset the even tenor of his constituent atoms, in prompting him to abstain from politics, and to advise his followers to live inconspicuously.

Like Habron and Demochares, Hegias of Sounion belonged to the second generation of a family of orators. He was of the Salaminian genos. In 302/1 he put to the vote a motion of thanks by Stratokles for a gift of grain.[21] A document of the end of the fourth century records the rental of a shrine by one of the lower-class cult groups called *orgeones* to another Salaminian, Diopeithes of Sounion.[22] An honorific decree of this genos from about this time testifies to the activity and prestige of the Salaminioi.[23]

The Eumolpids had less to be proud of: they admitted Poliorketes, most irregularly, into the Mysteries (302/1) by declaring April to be February in order to perform the preliminary initiation, and then following it with September to complete the job. The moderate democrats demonstrated against this gross and cynical irregularity. Though extraordinary measures were used to restore order,[24] the genos could argue that it acted only under pressure from the toady Stratokles; its prestige was too deep-rooted to topple as a result of this incident. Eumolpids and Kerykes continued to be active; they dedicated together a bronze statue of a hierophant, passed honorific decrees, supplied ambassadors, generals, and ephebes, and set up a calendar of sacrifices.[25]

One of the Hellenistic families who were very prominent is that of Echedemos and Mnesitheos of Kydathenaion, possibly of the genos of Kephalidai. The stemma can be traced for nine generations down into Augustan times [26] and presents the by now familiar pattern of activity: superintendents of festivals, dedicators, ambassadors, donors, victors in the games, suppliers of choruses. However there is no mention of any of those hereditary priesthoods which are our usual clue to membership in an aristocratic clan.

The last recorded act of Stratokles is a decree of 293/2 honoring a political rival.[27] This marks a reconciliation between the pro-Macedonian and the moderate democratic factions; the person honored was elected King Archon for this year.

Athens Crushed Between Macedon and Egypt

The coalition did not mean autonomy for Athens: the Macedonian garrison continued in the Peiraieus; Poliorketes, the erstwhile liberator, now King of Macedon, found it expedient to order the recall to Athens of oligarchs in exile; Ptolemy I of Egypt was willing enough to send gifts of grain and money, but did not care to risk dislodging the Macedonians from the city. Athens suffered four famines in seven years,[28] and the people were reduced to eating weeds. It was a dark time in more ways than one. In the

epigraphical record of the gene there is a gap of twenty
years. Yet cultural life went on: these were the years of
greatest activity for Zenon the Stoic, Epikouros, and
Krates; comedy flourished; Aratos, the astronomical poet,
visited Athens; the historians Timaios, Philochoros (certainly a gennetes), Demochares (possibly one), Diyllos (son
of the Atthidographer Phanodemos), Krateros (a collector
of inscriptions) were all active. Poliorketes' son and successor, Antigonos Gonatas, a pupil of Zenon, was a
philosopher-king.[29]

One of the ways in which the Athenians consoled themselves for their loss of independence was by passing decrees
honoring the fifty tribesmen (*prytaneis*) who during this
period served in tribal succession for a month at a time as
the executive committee of the Boule.[30] Regularly honored
were the treasurer and secretary of the prytany, the priest
of the eponymous hero of the tribe (who, if he did not
belong to the tribe in prytany, may have been the hereditary gentile priest of the hero in question [31]), the herald,
and other subordinate functionaries. In the middle years of
the third century the herald year after year was Eukles,
son of Philokles of Trinemeia. The office was hereditary
in his family, and makes plausible the conjecture that he
was a Keryx by genos as well as by profession.[32] We know
the name of the hierophant in 274/3: he was Chairetios of
Eleusis.[33] (Eumolpids often came from the deme where the
Mysteries were celebrated, Kerykes never: the inference is
that the former were the older genos, the latter Athenian
intruders, perhaps dating from no earlier than the seventh
century.)

The year 271/0 was the year of Epikouros' death and of
the honors for Demochares, in which mention of the kings
of Macedon was adroitly avoided in order not to give offense
to the moderate democrats.[34] The most important of these
is Phaidros of Sphettos, another of those equivocal figures
whose record is that of a typical gennetes, but whose gentile affiliation, if any, is unknown. He was honored, probably in 266/5,[35] as general (as his grandfather had been),

envoy to Ptolemy I, manager of games and sacrifices (as was his son after him), and generous donor (a man who kept the city "free, democratic and independent"—a pathetically meaningless series of epithets at a time when Athens depended for her very existence on the favor of a Ptolemy or an Antigonos).

A clansman, Chremonides, of the deme Aithalidai and the clan of the Praxiergidai, was responsible for a disastrous war which was initiated by a treaty with Sparta (265/4), traditionally the friend of the Athenian aristocracy.[36] His aim was to expel the Macedonian garrison from the Peiraieus through alliance with Ptolemy II Philadelphos. However the Spartan ally proved undependable, and Ptolemy's naval superiority was useless without a land force to cooperate in the relief of Athens. Chremonides accordingly surrendered (261/0). The Macedonians stationed a garrison in Athens itself, and installed a subservient government, one of whose members was the grandson of Demetrios of Phaleron.[37] For a generation Athens endured Macedonian rule.

Athens a Macedonian Puppet: 263–229

Since the pro-Macedonian faction was composed of propertied men, we naturally find gennetai in the government. A descendant of Harmodios and Aristogeiton, Anacharsis, son of Proxenos of Aphidna, moved a decree in 250/49;[38] a member of the Salaminioi, Hegesandros of Sounion, was councillor for Leontis in mid-century;[39] and about the same time an Eteoboutad, Niketes of Pergase, contributed to the support of the state and was superintendent of the Mysteries.[40]

After the middle of the century we find the first mention of the family of the brothers Eurykleides and Mikion of Kephisia, Eteoboutads in the noble tradition of Lykourgos. Under their leadership in the last quarter of the century, Athens was to enjoy the greatest measure of independence vouchsafed her in the Hellenistic Age. The brothers were

realistic enough to know that Athenian autonomy depended
upon the friendship of the great powers—first Egypt, and
then Rome. Polybios calls this indecent adulation, but he
was no friend to Athens. The brothers diplomatically connected their priesthood of the Demos and Graces with
that of Ptolemy III Euergetes (246–221) and his wife
Berenike,[41] after whom they were to name a new Attic
tribe, Ptolemais (229) and a deme, Berenikidai. The priest
was either Eurykleides I or Mikion II. The family relation-
ships are sufficiently important and complicated to be set
forth in a stemma, in accordance with which the various
members of the family will be numbered as they appear
in the succeeding narrative.

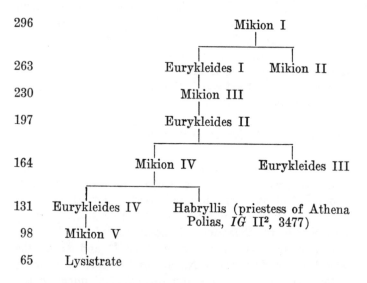

296			Mikion I	
263			Eurykleides I	Mikion II
230			Mikion III	
197			Eurykleides II	
164		Mikion IV		Eurykleides III
131	Eurykleides IV		Habryllis (priestess of Athena Polias, *IG* II², 3477)	
98	Mikion V			
65	Lysistrate			

The richest land in Attika is the central plain, the
Mesogeia, of which Eurykleides' and Mikion's deme,
Kephisia, forms a part. The members of the propertied
classes who lived there sometimes acted as a political entity
and passed decrees. The orator of one of these, Amynomachos, son of Philokrates of Bate, was closely enough
associated with the intelligentsia and gene to be mentioned

in Epikouros' will.[42] The person honored in Amynomachos' decree, Polyeuktos, son of Lysistratos of Bate, was superintendent of sacrifices and of a procession in honor of Herakles; as father of a priestess of Athena Polias, he, like Eurykleides and Mikion, was an Eteoboutad.[43] The clan made dynastic marriages; one of the daughters was married to an influential foreigner, Diogenes,[44] commandant of the Peiraieus garrison in 235; she did not lose her citizenship, and her descendants in turn became priestesses of Athena Polias.

Eumolpids as well as Eteoboutads figure in the decrees just after mid-century. The orator of a decree of about 248/7, Thrasyphon, son of Hierokleides of Xypete, was probably a Eumolpid, because he figures also as orator in in a decree (described by Meritt as in "characteristic letters of about 230 B.C.") in which the Eumolpids and Kerykes honor the hierophant.[45]

But Eurykleides I and Mikion II emerge more and more as the dominant figures of the period. They appear in a list of contributors now dated by Meritt as early 247/6.[46] About 230 we find Mikion II as agonothetes and Eurykleides I as hoplite general,[47] an office to which he was repeatedly re-elected; an honorific decree to him as general was passed by the Sounion detachment about the same time.[48]

The city of which Eurykleides and Mikion were increasingly assuming the leadership was to be freer than it had been for two generations, but more circumscribed, too, in its politics and its economy. As the inscriptions cited show, the loyalty of citizens was now divided between the state— a shadow of its former self—and the bewildering variety of semipublic or private organizations—gene, orgeones, and the rest. It was still a cultural center, but the culture did not filter down very far from the top, and Athens' preeminence was now reduced to one area, philosophy. Before long the Stoics were to devote themselves to the education of aristocratic Romans, with an interesting cross-fertilization of the two cultures as a result.[49]

The Regime of Eurykleides and Mikion: 229–196

In 229 Gonatas' son Demetrios II died, and Eurykleides decided to secede from Macedon. Diogenes, commandant in the Peiraieus, who (as we have seen) had married into Eurykleides' genos, concurred, on condition that 150 talents be found to pay off the troops. Interested parties in and out of Athens, probably including Ptolemy III Euergetes, made up the sum. Thus Athens was free of occupying troops for the first time in two generations.[50] The grateful Athenians passed a decree in praise of Eurykleides and his brother, in which they recognized the contribution of the pair to the safety of the city and the defense of Athens.[51] Eurykleides' contribution included no fewer than seven talents for the revival of the games as well as unspecified sums for replanting the long-neglected fields of Attika, paying off Diogenes' troops, dredging the harbors and rebuilding the walls of the city and the Peiraieus. Some of this was accomplished with Mikion's help. The decree also mentions diplomatic activity: Eurykleides' policy, which Polybios so despised, was complete isolation but peace and friendship with everybody, as exemplified in the surviving text of a pact with Kyrene.[52] Eurykleides' solicitude for the reseeding of Attika is what we might expect from a son of the Mesogeia. While he, like Perikles, ran Athens by virtue of repeated re-elections to the generalship, his partisans had themselves elected to the archonship. A nearly complete list of archons 229/8–213/2 survives: men from the Mesogeia held the top three posts eighteen times, townsmen ten, and men from coastal demes only five.[53]

An ancient Baedeker, Herakleides the Critic, has preserved for us a priceless glimpse of the Athens of Eurykleides and Mikion as it was about 205.[54] Eurykleides' reseeding has borne fruit, for the land is all cultivated, but hunger ever threatens and there is a water shortage. Though streets are crooked and most houses unimpressive, there still exist Perikles' Odeion, Lykourgos' theater, the

Parthenon, and Peisistratos' Olympieion, still unfinished (but destined to be worked on again in another generation by a Roman architect commissioned by Antiochos IV of Syria). Philosophers teach in the gymnasia, wooded and grassy parks. Banquets of all sorts, many snares and recreations of the spirit, unceasing shows abound. Sculptors flourish, but so do courtesans ("a pleasant destruction") and informers. Perhaps it is the circle of Eurykleides and Mikion who are "great-souled, simple in their manners, reliable custodians of friendship, . . . keen art critics, unwearying patrons of plays, concerts and lectures." Yet there are among the populace "inquisitive gossips, insincere, prone to blackmail and to pry into the private affairs of strangers"—the perennial Greek curiosity, as old as Odysseus, yet as new as St. Paul, and tomorrow.

This whole view implies the blessings of peace, for which the Athenians had Eurykleides and Mikion to thank. But their pursuit of alliances involved them with Attalos I of Pergamon, who was welcomed to Athens with great pomp in 200—priests and priestesses lining the streets on both sides and a new tribe named for him.[55] Attalos was involved with Rome against Philip V of Macedon, and Philip had made Attika suffer by destroying crops and orchards and, with unpardonable vandalism, hacking to pieces the marble monuments in the demes.[56] Shortly afterward, probably in 197/6, Eurykleides and Mikion died within a few months of each other, poisoned, gossip said, at Philip's instigation.[57] The Athenians erased the name of Macedon from their monuments; they were to move henceforth in the orbit of Rome.[58]

The Tory Democracy: 196–166

The generation between the proclamation by the Roman proconsul Flamininus of the freedom of Greece (196) and the Roman assignment of Delos to Athens (166) has been well called by Ferguson the age of the "Tory democracy."[59] The members of its ruling class were still an astute

and liberal aristocracy, propertied men, "trained in the
school of Eurykleides and Mikion,"[60] and therefore quick
to recognize the value of friendship with Rome. Eurykleides' son, Mikion III, was one of them, Echedemos of
Kydathenaion another. They revived the practice of setting
up expensive grave monuments, which had been in abeyance
since the sumptuary legislation of Demetrios of Phaleron.
Their names appear, among others, with related symbols,
on the New Style coinage which runs in an unbroken series
for 110 years from Flamininus' proclamation to the sack
of Athens by Sulla.[61] It may be that the symbols keyed to
the moneyer and/or his gens which begin to appear on
Roman coinage about 187, were inspired by the Athenian
model.[62] One can identify with greater or lesser certainty
five gennetai among the Athenian mint-magistrates of
196–166: Niketes of Pergase (Eteoboutad) in 193/2;
Ammonios of Anaphlystos (Keryx) in 182/1 and 180/79;[63]
Adeimantos of Ikaria (Eteoboutad or Phytalidai) 179/8;[64]
Echedemos (Kephalidai?) in 170/69,[65] and Mikion III
(Eteoboutad) in 169/8. This placing of names on coins is
described by Ferguson as a "quasi-monarchical privilege,"
which the Pisistratids had been the last to use.[66] And the
use of symbols harks back to the *Wappenmünzen* of the
sixth-century aristocrats: the old cicada appears in 185/4,
and the forepart of a horse in 177/6.

These wealthy men had the support of the Roman senate.
Echedemos had been an envoy to the Scipios in 190/89.[67]
For Roman philhellenes like Flamininus or Scipio, the con-
tact with Greeks was pleasant enough, but for austere Puri-
tans like the notorious Greek-hater, Cato the Elder, Greeks
were exasperating with their expansiveness, their love of
discussion and controversy, their delight in bargaining and
shady deals.[68]

Under the Tory democrats one would not expect the
gene to lose their religious prerogatives, and the prytany
lists prove that they did not. We know of four priests of
the eponymous heroes of the tribes in this period who
probably were gennetai. A priest who served the tribe

Erechtheis, but was not a member of that tribe, probably was an Eteoboutad, in view of that clan's monopoly of the Erechtheum cult. Such a one was Kalliades of Aigilia, priest of the eponymos for Erechtheis in about 190.[69] In 178/7 Thrasippos, son of Kallias of Gargettos—a deme of the tribe Aigeis—was priest of Hippothontis;[70] sometime between 165 and 150 his son Kallias was priest of the tribe Erechtheis.[71] What the two tribes had in common was a connection with Poseidon: Hippothoon was Poseidon's son, Erechtheus one of his cult titles. Hence Thrasippos and Kallias may also have been Eteoboutads. In 173/2 Adeimantos of Ikaria was priest of Attalis.[72] Ikaria is a deme of this tribe, but the trident device chosen by Adeimantos when he was mint-magistrate suggests, as we saw, a gentile affiliation for him with either the Eteoboutads or the Phytalidai.

A government without real power will find consolation in religious observances, and the prytany-decrees are remarkable for their piety.[73] But the sacrifices are made to gods who have no gentile cult: Apollo Prostaterios and Artemis Boulaia; Artemis Phosphoros, who appeared to Thrasyboulos on his return from Phyle; Athena Archegetis, who appears on New Style bronze coinage (without magistrates' names) holding an owl in her outstretched hand.[74]

The Eumolpids and Kerykes who, as *spondophoroi*, toured foreign parts with invitations to the Mysteries, acted as intelligence officers. They made reports, for example, of foreigners kindly disposed toward Athens, men like the nephew of the Stoic Chrysippos, who had studied in Athens and held open house for Athenians visiting Antioch; the Athenians honored him in a decree of 196/5.[75]

The orator of the decree is also named on one of the most illuminating documents of the Tory democracy, a list of contributors (183/2) to an unknown cause.[76] This list includes names for a cross-section of the ruling class, complete with wives and children, and their well-wishers abroad—from Tanagra, Tenos, the Chersonese, Kyzikos, Mytilene, Rhodes, Paphos, and Seleukeia. Echedemos of

Kydathenaion leads the list, which seems to be arranged
in order of prestige; Mikion III comes second. The
hierophant Amynomachos is there, and the family of
Habron of Bate. The activities of the contributors, their
ancestors and descendants give an excellent idea of what
the propertied citizens regarded as proper civic activity
in Hellenistic and Roman Athens, and what was expected
of them. They commissioned statues, wrote comedies, acted
as treasurers, superintended everything from affairs on the
island of Delos—when it became Athenian—to processions
and the distribution of the dole, acted as ambassadors and
proxenoi, were elected generals and thesmothetai, and went
on pious pilgrimages to Delphi. They were a clique and a
privileged class, but they paid for their privileges with a
real and generous sense of civic responsibility.

The Eurykleides-Mikion families are dominant in this
whole generation. In the Great Panathenaia of 182/1 and
178/7, which were particularly splendid, Mikion IV and
his grandson won chariot victories, as did Eurykleides II,
and Arketos I and Mnesitheos III, sons of Echedemos III
of Kydathenaion; Kallias, son of Thrasippos of Gargettos,
whom we have already met as a priest, won as a bareback
rider. They kept very distinguished company; among the
other successful competitors were Ptolemy V Epiphanes,
King of Egypt, and Eumenes II of Pergamon and his
brother.[77] In 172/1 Mikion IV, along with Echedemos III
and others, contributed to the building of towers on the
Long Walls.[78] And the Agora excavations turned up the
base of a statue dedicated by Eurykleides II in 171/0.[79]

The circle of Eurykleides and Mikion included Karaichos
of Halai, one of the contributors of 183/2. In 163/2 he was
second mint-magistrate with an Antiochos, perhaps the boy
king of Syria who won a Panathenaic victory in this year.
(Eleven years earlier this boy's father, Antiochos IV
Epiphanes, had, as we saw, resumed on an imposing scale
the building of the Olympieion, begun by Peisistratos
nearly 400 years before.) In any case Antiochos, the colleague of Karaichos, had as his coin symbol the Seleucid

elephant.[80] Thus the ruling families of Athens had their connections with Seleucids as well as with Ptolemies and Attalids, making Athens, for all her political impotence, a truly international center which monarchs delighted to honor.

In the war against Perseus of Macedon, which Paulus won at Pydna in 168, the Tory democracy had been unswervingly loyal to Rome. They demanded, and in 166 won, their reward; the Roman senate granted them Delos, which had been lost to Athens under Demetrios of Phaleron in 314. Athenian *klerouchoi* were settled in Delos and took over the entire administration of the island; hereafter the familiar names of Athenians of the best families appear regularly as administrators and priests on the island. The wretched Delians were deported wholesale to Achaia. The wheel had come full circle; this island which Athens had lost at the beginning of the Hellenistic Age and in which the Periklean Empire had found the center of its growth, was once more in the hands of Perikles' descendants. The Romans declared Delos a free port, but many an Athenian fortune must have been made in the notorious Delian slave trade, and on the island, members of Athens' first families became priests of the various exotic Syrian and Egyptian cults which had their temples there.[81]

Most histories of Athens end with the deaths of Demosthenes and Aristotle; most histories of Greece in the Hellenistic Age concentrate on the kingdoms of Alexander's successors in Egypt, Syria, and Macedon. This chapter will have been of value if it reminds us of Ferguson's brilliant reconstruction from *disiecta membra* of Athenian history in the Hellenistic Age; his reconstruction has been revised here to take account of the role of the gene in keeping Athenian cultural, religious, and to some extent even political life alive in a world which for centuries to come was to be dominated by Rome.

Three

From the Reacquisition of Delos to the Battle of Actium (166–31)

For the four generations between the reacquisition of Delos and the battle of Actium there is more evidence than ever before for the importance of the gene—especially the Kerykes, Eumolpids, Eteoboutadai, and Salaminioi (but other clans, previously less prominent, emerge)—in cult and festivals, administration civil and military, and in finance. The senatorial aristocracy in Rome supported the aristocracy in Athens, and vice versa. Increasingly, events in Italy and Sicily controlled the course of events in Athens and Delos: slave revolts in the west had their repercussions in Laureion and on Delos; the support by the Athenian demos of Mithridates of Pontus against Rome led to the disastrous sack of Athens by Sulla. After the sack, Athens revived, but her leaders, whether aristocrats or demos, showed a fatal proclivity for supporting the losing side in Rome's civil wars: first Pompey against Caesar, then Brutus and Cassius against Antony and Octavian, finally Antony against Octavian. But Athenian intellectual prestige and artistic competence proved useful to the conqueror: in the end, *Graecia capta ferum victorem cepit:* the symbols are Athenian sculpture on the Ara Pacis, and the upstart temple of Rome and Augustus beside the Periklean Parthenon on the Acropolis. The traditions of the Athenian aristocracy do not suffer in the comparison.[1]

The Gene from 166 to 145

Down to the Sullan sack the New Style coins with their magistrates' names and symbols continue to provide valuable evidence of the activity of gennetai. For the first twenty years after the re-establishment of the Delian cleruchy the evidence is positive and indicates the especial prominence of the Kerykes.[2] Our ability to recognize Kerykes from the Roman period results from extrapolations back from a late first-century decree—here called the Mélanges Bidez decree—of the Boule and demos, now in the Eleusis Museum, honoring the torchbearer—a religious office hereditary, as we have seen, in the genos of the

49

Kerykes—Themistokles son of Theophrastos of Hagnous. The decree mentions incidentally, with patronymics, fifty members of the clan, whose ancestries stretch back into the third century B.C., and whose descendants extend to the end of the first century A.D.[3]

Another genos whose members we can identify on the coins is that of Lykourgos, the Eteoboutadai, because of the frequent mention in inscriptions of identifiable priestesses of Athena Polias, which were hereditary in this clan. As may be seen on the following page, we are able to combine information to identify certain gennetai among the mint-magistrates of 159/8–145/4. The cicada symbol goes back to the sixth-century *Wappenmünzen;* the Dioskouroi, heavenly twins, are appropriate for brothers; the three Graces refer to Eurykleides' priesthood; the two torches to the hereditary Keryx office of torchbearer; the prow with trophy to the earlier Themistokles' victory at Salamis. Apollo Delios refers to the first magistrate's priesthood on Delos; he has demonstrable connections with Dionysodoros of Deiradiotai, whose homonymous descendant is mentioned in the *Mélanges Bidez* decree. The Triptolemos symbol is connected with Eleusis: the second magistrate may be an ancestor of Dositheos, son of Kleomenes of Marathon, who appears as "bearer of the sacred stone" on the *Mélanges Bidez* decree.

We have evidence other than coins of the importance of the Eteoboutadai in this period. Protagoras son of Niketes of Pergase was honored as priest of Asklepios in 165/4: he probably belongs to the genos, for his granddaughter Chrysis was priestess of Athena Polias in 106/5.[11] Elegiac couplets of the mid-century celebrate the priestess Philotera and her descent from Lykourgos.[12] A little later, an inscription is dated in the term of office of the priestess Habryllis, daughter of Mikion IV of Kephisia.[13] Lykourgos' wife (as we saw) was the daughter of Habron of Bate, whose family was, therefore, connected with the Eteoboutad genos by marriage, even though we have no record of any member of it who held the canonical post of priestess of Athena

Date	Mint-Magistrate 1	Mint-Magistrate 2	Genos	Symbol
159/8	Lysandros	Glaukos [4]	brothers, Eteoboutadai	cicada
156/5	Mikion IV	Eurykleides III [5]	brothers, Eteoboutadai	**Dioskouroi**
154/3	Eurykleides III	Ariarathes [6]	first mint-magistrate, Eteoboutad	three Graces
150/49	Ammonios	Kallias [7]	first mint-magistrate, Keryx	two torches
149/8	Themistokles	Theopompos [8]	first mint-magistrate, Lykomid	prow with trophy
148/7	Sokrates	Dionysodoros [9]	first mint-magistrate, Eteoboutad second mint-magistrate, Keryx	Apollo Delios
145/4	Eumareides	Kleomenes [10]	second mint-magistrate, Keryx	**Triptolemos**

Polias. But in the second century, five generations of the
family achieved prominence in the traditional aristocratic
ways. In the first generation, Habron III, son of Kallias,
contributed money to an unknown cause in 183/2 and, at
a ripe age, was treasurer of his prytany in 162/1 and
hieropoios of the Athenaia in 156/5.[14] In the second, his
son Ophelas served as a cavalry commander in the Theseia
of about 158/7 and, about mid-century, contributed to the
building of the Peiraieus theater.[15] In the third generation,
Habron's grandson, Habron IV, won the boys' pankration
in the Theseia of 161/0, and the boxing about 158/7; another grandson, Euktemon, won the junior boxing in the
same year; a third grandson, Drakon son of Ophelas, won
the horse race.[16] In the fourth generation, Habron's great-
grandsons, Habron V and Kallias V, near the end of the
century, joined other aristocratic young men in the pilgrimage to Delphi which was called the Pythais;[17] they
are listed as belonging to a specific genos called Eupatridai.
And in the fifth generation, Habron's great-great-grand-
daughter was in 108/7 among the *ergastinai*, little girls of
good family who wove the peplos for Athena.[18]

Just before mid-century the Eleusinian priestly gene
cooperated closely with the Athenian demos in honoring
both their own and foreign benefactors. In 153/2 they
jointly honored the hierophant Aristokles of Perithoidai,
during whose over thirty years in office many sacrifices
which had been held in abeyance for years were restored.
The mover of the decree, Amynomachos son of Eukles of
Halai, was the hierophant's brother (presumably adoption
is involved, since their demotics are different) and was
himself hierophant later.[19] In another joint decree of about
the same date, the Kerykes and Eumolpids, together with
the demos, honored Philonides and his sons Philonides and
Dikaiarchos of Laodikaia with honorary citizenship and
a statue in the precinct of the Demos and Graces. Dikaiarchos had served the Delphians at the court of Antiochos
IV Epiphanes, while the younger Philonides had converted
the monarch to Epicureanism.[20] The cosmopolitan gennetai

of the period apparently saw no inconsistency between tenets of the Garden and the Eleusinian Mysteries. In the Panathenaia of either 162/1 or 158/7, the Keryx Ammonios, son of Ammonios of Anaphlystos, was a fellow victor with Antiochos V Eupator, son of Epiphanes.[21] Gennetai and philosophers joined in honoring kings and Romans in festivals. In 152/1 the Romaia were celebrated in Athens and Delos, and (for the last time in the century) the Ptolemaia in Athens. Over sixty commissioners for the latter are listed, among them Panaitios of Rhodes and other Stoic philosophers; there also appears for the first time a gennetes whose descendants were to be potent in Athens for a hundred years, Medeios of the Peiraieus, who traced his descent from Lykourgos; four generations later another Medeios was Eumolpid expounder of the mysteries (*exegetes*).[22] The gennetai consorted with the lowly as well as with the high and mighty. In a list of *eranistai* (picnickers—a humble dining club) of the mid-century, among foreigners and slaves there appears the name of Diodoros of Sounion, of the Salaminian genos.[23]

The Gene in Temporary Eclipse (144/3–129/8)

In 146 the Romans sacked Corinth, and the Italians who had been in business there transferred their offices to Delos, where there was a flourishing slave trade, and God and Mammon prospered side by side. Property values promptly rose, and property became concentrated in the hands of a few Athenians. In the 140's and the 130's, the known Athenian families who held both property and priesthoods on the island were apparently businessmen; recognizable gennetai are rare. When we combine with this the observation that between 144/3 and 129/8 we can identify only one gennetes among the mint-magistrates on Athenian New Style coins, it begins to look as though the aristocratic Athenian ruling class was in temporary eclipse during those years.[24] A list of Delian gymnasiarchs which includes the period has only one certainly gentile name, while two

lists of Athenian *epimeletai,* dated 130–120, contain the
names of many men of wealth (their ancestors and descendants appear on lists of contributors), but few if any
are *gennetai.*[25]

Of course the gene did not, in this period or ever, lose
their religious prerogatives: two priests of the eponymoi
were gennetai, the Keryx Ammonios of Anaphlystos for
Antiochis in 140/39, and the Eteobutad Thrasippos son of
Kallias of Gargettos in 135/4.[26] And in 138/7 was revived
the Pythais-pilgrimage to Delphi in which many gennetai
participated with éclat. The names of the pilgrims are
inscribed on the south wall of the Athenian Treasury at
Delphi: they include *theoroi, pythaistai, kanephorai,*
knights, musicians, poets, actors, and the guild of Dionysiac
technitai, which, like the gene, passed its own honorific
decrees (it enjoyed immunity from taxation and military
service). A decree of 129/8, the year before the second
Pythais, prescribes renewed pomp for Apollo's cult in
Athens; it exudes aristocratic piety, prospering under the
protection of the Roman peace.[27]

Eupatrid Revival (129/8–87/6)

The eupatrid political eclipse was of short duration. The
political reaction against the *populares* in Rome, which set
in after Tiberius Gracchus' murder in 133, may have been
reflected in Athens; at any rate from 129/8 to the Sullan
sack in 86, eupatrid names abound in the key posts: among
the *epimeletai* who governed Delos, the mint-magistrates,
and the archons. Ex-archons went into the Areiopagos;
about the beginning of this period, the Herald of the
Areiopagos and the Hoplite General begin to assume such
importance that they have been compared to the consuls
in Rome. A list of contributors of 125/4 is crammed with
eupatrid names.[28] The Pythais was sent to Delphi three
times: in 128/7, 106/5 (a particularly splendid pilgrimage)
and in 97/6. In 103/2 another Pythais went to Delos. All
these pilgrimages were supported by eupatrid participation

and subsidy. Athens' intellectual prestige was high in these years: a constant stream of Romans came to study, admire and receive honors. For the Panathenaia, eupatrid maidens wove Athena's peplos, and had their names solemnly recorded on stone. On the surface, everything seemed for the best in the best of all possible worlds; only the slave revolts struck a sinister note. If the demos had not flirted disastrously with Mithridates, Sulla might not have been so vindictive, and Athens' Indian summer might have lasted another generation.

Gennetai now monopolized the superintendency of Delos. The family of Ammonios of Anaphlystos (Kerykes) held the office four times, sometimes for longer than a year at a time: in 129/8, 111/0, 107/6, and sometime between 105 and 103. The Eteoboutad-Eumolpid family of Medeios of the Peiraieus also held it four times: Diogenes son of Aropos in 115/4; Sarapion of Melite (an upstart who married into the family) in 100/99; the most prominent of all the Medeioi in 98/7 (in his long career he went twice on the Pythais to Delphi, was archon four times, hoplite-general, trierarch, gymnasiarch, *agonothetes,* mint-magistrate twice, head of the state bank on Delos, and priest of Poseidon Erechtheus); and Aropos, son of Glaukos of the Peiraieus, in 94/3 (elegiacs celebrate him for subservience to the Romans). Drakon, son of Ophelas of Bate (Eteoboutad by marriage, and Eupatrid, as we have seen), was *epimeletes* in 112/11. Dionysios, son of Nikon of Pallene, held the office in 110/9; in the same year his son Nikon dedicated a statue to the Roman proconsul Ser. Cornelius Lentulus; another son and a grandson were epimeletai of the island, about 80 and in 48/7, and a great-great-great grandson was hoplite-general under Claudius. The family is guaranteed Keryx by the *Mélanges Bidez* inscription. Theodotos son of Diodoros of Sounion (Salaminioi) was epimeletes in 102/1, having been priest of the Syrian Goddess Hagne Aphrodite about 111/0. And Demeas son of Hikesios of Halai, another Keryx, held the office in 90/89.[29]

In mint-magistracies, the gene predominate. Out of forty-one issues between 128/7 and 88/7, members of gene are represented in twenty-eight; they held both magistracies in fourteen issues. The Kerykes held the post twenty-eight times (with some iteration in office); other gene—Eumolpids, Eteoboutadai, Gephyraioi, Philleidai, and Erysichthonidai—account for thirteen more. The aristocratic mint-magistrate, before or after he discharged this liturgy, served as archon, basileus, polemarch, hoplite-general, herald of the Areiopagos, superintendent of Delos, agonothetes or priest. The symbols chosen are often a clue to the magistrates' gentile affiliation: Demeter, Triptolemos, the herald Hermes or his winged caduceus for the Eumolpids or Kerykes; the old cicada symbol from the sixth-century *Wappenmünzen;* a pair of brothers chose the Gephyraioi Harmodios and Aristogeiton. Consanguinity as a principle was more frequent in these years than ever before: eleven out of the twenty-eight pairs were in some way related: fathers and sons, brothers, or brothers-in-law, for example; and there were also interrelations by marriage between pairs of magistrates. In sum, the mint-magistrates were, even more in this period than formerly, a civic-minded and philanthropic aristocracy, and behaved as such.[30]

Archons' names are hard to identify as eupatrid because they are usually recorded without patronymic and demotic, but Demochares of 108/7 and Argeios of 98/7 were probably Kerykes; Medeios (101/0, 91/0–89/8—a dictatorship) had, as we have seen, both Eteoboutad and Eumolpid connections; Menedemos of 92/1 probably belonged to the Philleidai, and several others are less certain but possible.[31]

But archonships were valuable chiefly for the entrance into the Areiopagos which an archonship guaranteed. The Herald of the Areiopagos is first mentioned in 129/8,[32] but apparently achieved maximum prestige from the fifties of the first century B.C. The other important office, that of hoplite-general, was more ornamental than useful, now that Athens had neither a citizen-army nor wars to fight;

but mercenary troops were kept on the watch against pirate forays, and the general Herakleitos—patronymic and demotic unknown—put down the revolt of the slaves in the Laureion silver mines in 130.[33] According to a list of contributors to the Delian Pythais (103/2–97/6), the hoplite-general made the largest donation; he is listed ahead of the archon of the year. Three of the names are familiar and are either of gennetai or of those having gentile connections: Ammonios of Anaphlystos in 103/2, Sarapion of Melite in 102/1 and 98/7, Medeios of the Peiraieus in 99/8.[34]

What is meant by the ornamental quality of Athenian military exercises at this time is illustrated by a list of activities of ephebes (127/6), including many aristocratic names, which recur on the list of young men who escorted the second Pythais to Delphi; [35] their younger sisters wove the Panathenaic peplos for Athena. Among the activities, gentile piety and antiquarianism are marked: sacrifices to the gods and *Euergetai* (meaning the Romans); pilgrimages to all the shrines, including Delphi; sacrifices on the borders to the gods of Attika; sailing to Salamis for the Aianteia. Military exercises, apart from escort duty, were confined to a prize drill at the Theseia, and attending the ekklesia in armor.

In a list of names of about 125/4, Kerykes, Eumolpids, and Philleidai so predominate that it must relate to the Eleusinian Mysteries. Hierophants or priests of Demeter are mentioned four times; there are six Kerykes and two Philleidai. Two descendants of the famous Philaid Miltiades are named, three members of the family of Eurykleides and Mikion, and also the ubiquitous Medeios of the Peiraieus, and his kinsmen, Aropos and Sarapion of Melite.[36]

The pietistic antiquarianism of the time is reflected in the mention of three rare gene. About 117, the Bakchiadai set up an altar in the precinct of Dionysos, naming two archons of their genos, not upstarts, for their grandfather had been rich enough to be a contributor in 183/2.[37] One of the pilgrims in the third and most splendid Pythais to

Delphi (106/5) is specified as belonging to the Euneidai,
a clan of official musicians, who shared the priesthood of
Dionysios Melpomenos with the important guild of Dionysiac technitai. The family survived the Sullan sack: a son
is named high on a list of contributors to the building of
a gymnasium about 50.[38] And an inscription of about 100
may be restored as referring to the Kynneidai, hereditary
priests of Apollo Kynneios; the gennetes named was also
priest of Apollo Patroios.[39] This Athens of the gennetai
claimed in an inscription of 117 set up in both Delphi and
Athens, to be ''the inaugurator of all human blessings, the
guide of men from the life of beasts to gentle culture, the
establisher in fact of the social organism altogether . . .
through the dissemination of her Mysteries, which pro-
claimed abroad the sovereign value of mutual aid and con-
fidence among men; and also through passing on to others
the education and laws with which the gods had dowered
her . . . Though grain had been given her as her special
property, she had made it everybody's heritage. She was,
besides, the originator of music and dramatic art, the
founder and developer of tragedy and comedy.''[40]
This high-flown language was intended to buttress the
claim to special privilege of the Dionysiac technitai, but
also reflected in it are the claims to notice of the Eleusinian
priestly gene, and the fame of Athens as a university for
Roman aristocratic youth; indeed the inscription refers to
the Romans as ''universal benefactors'' (*koinoi euergetai*).

Two great Roman orators were among the visitors to
Athens: Crassus in 110/9; [41] and Marcus Antonius, the
triumvir's grandfather, in 103/2. Antonius was on his way
to suppress Cilician pirates. His visit followed shortly
upon the second slave revolt, which moved the Athenian
ruling class to take stern measures. Ferguson's suggestion
that Antonius supported this ''oligarchic revolution'' is
ingenious, but his allegation that ''the democracy was
overthrown, and a government of businessmen took its
place'' will not hold.[42] Power, indeed, was concentrated in
few hands during the years between 103/2 and 97/6. But

Athens had not had consecutive years of democratic leadership since the 130's, and the ruling group of 103/2 and after (Medeios and the rest) were, demonstrably, not *parvenus*—Sarapion being admittedly an exception. Rather they were men who in many cases could trace their pedigrees back to the fourth century. A decree now passed to standardize weights, measures, and coinage was certainly good for business in Athens and on Delos. However, the business was one in which gennetai were engaged, and the commissioner in charge of the reform was the eupatrid Diodoros of Halai, whose family had connections both with the Kerykes and the Gephyraioi.[43]

The best prosopographical source for the aristocratic composition of the government at the turn of the century is the list of contributors to the first enneaeteric Delian Pythais, arranged by years from 103/2 through 97/6.[44] Of the 111 persons whose names are legible on the stone, twenty-three are certainly, probably, or possibly gennetai.[45] Of these, eight have pedigrees which go back to 166 or earlier. Nonetheless all but one or two of the twenty-three families survived the Sullan sack with unimpaired prestige. Fourteen families still matter in the first Christian century, six in the second. This prestige was largely political: for over 250 years, from 154/3 to A.D. 100, no generation of Athenian political life is without its representative from these key families. Eight out of eleven known hoplite-generals related to the 111 persons recorded on the stone were gennetai; so also ten out of sixteen superintendents of Delos, nine out of seventeen archons, three out of seven heralds of the Areiopagos. But the equal importance of herald and general, mentioned above, is not yet the rule between 103/2 and 97/6: the hoplite-general is mentioned ahead of the herald and contributes twice as much.

Since the inscription has a religious purpose, cult bulks large, but less among the gennetai listed than in their families. Only three of the gennetai were priests: one of Dionysos, the other two of Egyptian or Syrian deities. But in the twenty-three families religious activity was vigorous:

there are priests of Zeus Kynthios, Apollo, the Great Gods, Poseidon Erechtheus, Amynos, priestesses of Demeter and Athena, a subpriestess of Artemis, hierophants, a hierophantis, an exegetes, and numerous theoroi, ergastinai, and functionaries called *epi ta hiera* (vestrymen?). The twenty-three gennetai are related to sixteen mint-magistrates. Their record in the traditionally aristocratic enterprise of being great builders is not distinguished, but the Theophrastos who built on Delos in 126/5 the great agora which still survives was probably related to one of them, an Amynandrid. In the creative arts, aristocrats are more likely to be patrons than practitioners, but the leading figure of the whole group, Ammonios of Anaphlystos, hoplite-general in 103/2, had a brother who was a poet.

Adoptions figure largely in the group's family history, even where there were lineal descendants. The aim seems to have been to assure to the adopter the prestige of the priesthoods hereditary in the genos of the collateral line. This may explain the double genos of Medeios and the triple affiliation of Zenon of Marathon.

But politics was the most important activity: of the twenty-three families, eleven held political office. In this list, as often elsewhere, the Kerykes—twelve out of twenty-three—seem to hold pride of place, ranking as a *gens maior*, like the Cornelii in Rome.[46] In sum, this stone reveals aristocrats doing civic service at considerable personal expense in a difficult time. Athenian government as a *hypo tou protou andros arche* (government by the first citizen) was not confined to the Golden Age.

Another fruitful source of information about the prominence of gennetai toward the end of the century is the series of inscriptions honoring the ergastinai, who, as we saw, wove the peplos for Athena. Of seventy-two fathers' names legible or restorable on the stones, a plausible case can be made for fifteen as gennetai or connected with gennetai by marriage. The gene involved are the Eteoboutadai (four entries), Kerykes (five), Eumolpidai, Eupatridai (as a specific genos), Gephyraioi, Philaidai,

Erysichthonidai, Euneidai, and probably the Salaminioi and the infrequently mentioned Apheidantidai. Among the families are the familiar names of Kallias of Bate, Mikion of Kephisia, Zenon of Marathon, Sarapion of Melite, and Miltiades of Lakiadai.[47] The gene were prosperous: some of them had large families; Kallias of Bate had four children, Dionysios of Pallene five, Zenon of Marathon four, and Sarapion of Melite five. There is a higher proportion of eupatrid daughters among the ergastinai than there is of eupatrid sons among the ephebes, but in this generation both sexes had their moment of glory, and it was duly recorded.

The ruling class, Medeios and his circle, were creditors. The debtor demos could be saved only by the fall of Rome, and for this they looked to Mithridates of Pontos.[48] Athenian dedications to Mithridates have been found on Delos, and it is noteworthy that those who made them do not bear eupatrid names.[49] Medeios, against the pro-Mithridates democrats, resorted to coercion: public assembly was forbidden; his enemies complained that the temples were shut, the gymnasia idle, the lecture rooms empty; for an unprecedented three years (91/0–89/8) Medeios held the archonship as virtual dictator.[50] The demos sent the peripatetic philosopher Athenion to ask Mithridates' help; he returned triumphant, in a silver-footed litter, arrayed in purple and wearing the king's gold signet ring. The Dionysiac technitai escorted him, hailing him as the New Dionysos. Speaking from the bema built for Roman generals in front of the Stoa of Attalos, he called eupatrid rule "anarchy."[51] (When the eupatrids regained power, they labeled the democratic interlude "anarchy," and the allegation survives on stone to this day.) The demos elected him hoplite-general, and Athens again had a philosopher-king, as in the days of Demetrios of Phaleron. Medeios and his friends fled; the demos instituted a reign of terror with curfews imposed and passports required. Athenion despatched his lieutenant Apellikon with 1000 men to Delos, where the Italians ambushed them, killing 600 and making prisoners

of the rest. The result was Athenion's fall, and replacement
by the Stoic Aristion with Mithridates' backing. In the
summer of 87 Sulla, enraged by Mithridates' having in-
cited the Asiatic Greeks to slaughter 80,000 Italians, ar-
rived before Athens with 30,000 men. The trees in Plato's
Academy and Aristotle's Lykeion were felled to make siege
engines. There was famine, and the Athenians were reduced
to eating boiled leather. Antiquarians enumerated Athens'
past services; Sulla rejoined, "I have not come to learn
ancient history, but to punish rebels." In March of 86 the
city fell. Aristion and the ringleaders held out for a time
on the Akropolis, but were finally taken and executed. At
the intercession of Medeios and others, the rest were pardoned, and Athens returned to eupatrid rule: in 86/5 a
hierophant was archon.[52] Sulla shipped much loot to Rome,
including some columns from the Olympieion, and Apellikon's library, of which a part was the works of Aristotle
—ironically, it is to this seizure that we owe their preserva-
tion. In less than two years the peace and prosperity of a
century and a half had been annihilated.

From the Sullan Sack to Pharsalos (87/6–48)

From the Sullan sack to the battle of Pharsalos, Athenian
politics were unsettled. One index is the scrappy state of
the archon lists, which, almost unbroken from 499 until
now, suddenly show large gaps (for example, from 74/3
to 67/6). Another is Athens' loss of the right of independent coinage. The first step was large Sullan issues with
the ethnic and the magistrates' names vindictively sup-
pressed. Then silver ceased altogether, and only bronze
was coined. The coins which had been sound currency for
centuries ceased to exist, and Athenian aristocrats had one
less liturgy to discharge.[53] The demos hastened to make
amends to Sulla by dedicating a statue to him;[54] what is
less surprising is that the Areiopagos, always strongly
pro-Roman, did so also.[55] Games were instituted in his
honor, the Sylleia (83–78). The ephebe decree on which

they are mentioned has a strongly oligarchic flavor: the honors are decreed by the Boule alone, and the proclamation of crowns is made by the hoplite-general—who is mentioned in the first line, directly after the archon—and the herald of the Areiopagos.[56] A decree concerning the restoration of damaged temples and other buildings has been emended so that it now appears to date after the sack; here too eupatrid piety is conspicuous.[57]

There was a revival on Delos also. There the demos, no doubt in the hope of making the Romans forget that it had supported Mithridates, dedicated a statue to the Roman Lucius Caecilius Metellus, in the year of the superintendency of Protimos (son of Dositheos of Myrrhinoutta, who, as we saw, may have been a Salaminian by genos.)[58] In about 80, the Theseia were revived, perhaps the same fete then called the Sylleia in Athens: a Roman won the torch race, and the epimeletes was Hermaphilos son of Dionysios of Pallene, a Keryx.[59] Several inscriptions name another Keryx, Kallimachos of Leukonoe, as superintendent about 68/7.[60] If island installations were damaged in the pirate war of 79, there were funds for rapid rebuilding: the agora of the Italians was rebuilt in 78/7.[61]

In the pirate war Lucius Licinius Lucullus (cos. 74), Sulla's old lieutenant, earned Athenian gratitude. A dedication to him by the Athenian demos has been used to argue that Athens was a democracy at this time,[62] but another, by demos and Areiopagos together, damages the contention.[63] The Athenian aristocracy in these years continued to play its part in putting down piracy: an inscription of about 79 from the Peiraieus is engraved with nine crowns voted by various beneficiaries, including the Athenian Boule and demos together, to an unnamed admiral who was archon of the genos of the Kerykes.[64] The demos alone gave thanks to Gaius Valerius Triarius, who built a wall on Delos about 68/7 to protect it against pirates,[65] and after 63/2 the demos alone erected a statue to King Deiotaros of Galatia, who adroitly played both sides in Rome's civil wars.[66] However these examples by themselves are insufficient to prove that Athens was a democracy in these years, because Medeios, son of the dictator of 91–88, and himself a Eumolpid exegetes, was archon about 65/4,[67] and the Gephyraios, Diodoros son of Theophilos of Halai in 53/2.[68] In his archonship the demos and Boule jointly dedicated a statue of Appius Claudius Pulcher, Cicero's predecessor as proconsul of Cilicia, who built new propylaea at Eleusis.[69]

Roman desire for initiation enhanced the prestige of the Eleusinian priestly gene. An inscription of the period, not precisely datable, makes careful provision for preserving order at the Mysteries and implies the presence of large crowds.[70] The priestess of Demeter and Kore (about mid-century), Kleokrateia, was the daughter of Oinophilos of Aphidna, who had been king-archon before the sack; the family could trace its ancestry back to the fifth century.[71]

From 62/1 to 46/5 we have a solid block of firmly dated archons,[72] itself perhaps an indication that the archives were in orderly eupatrid hands. But, in addition, some of the archons were gennetai: Herodes, archon in 60/59, belonged to the Marathonian family of Kerykes whose most famous—and richest—member was the millionnaire philanthropist of Marcus Aurelius' time, Herodes Attikos; the earlier Herodes' son Eukles may have been archon in 46/5.[73] Diodoros, archon in 53/2, we have already mentioned; his successor Lysandros was, though adopted by Apolexis of Oion (nephew of the ill-fated admiral Apellikon), in fact the son of Lysandros of the Peiraieus, who belonged to Medeios' family.[74] Furthermore, we have the complete roster of the magistrates of 56/5: the herald of the Areiopagos was the Eumolpid Theophemos son of Metrodoros of Kydathenaion; the archon's herald, Eudemos son of Gorgippos of Melite, was Keryx by clan as well as by profession, since his son was listed on the *Mélanges Bidez* decree as herald of Pythian Apollo.[75] Oinophilos son of Syndromos of Steiria, treasurer of his prytany about mid-century, belonged to a Eumolpid family of great prestige; to the same generation belonged Kallikratides son of Syndromos of Trikorynthos, who adopted Oinophilos'

son, and made his mark as hoplite-general and herald of
the Boule and demos later in the century.[76]

Pharsalos to Actium (48–31)

In the civil war in which Pompey was defeated at
Pharsalos in 48, the Athenian eupatrids, like the optimates,
their counterparts in Rome, supported Pompey,[77] no doubt
remembering how he had swept the pirates from the
Aegean. But Caesar pardoned Athens, "because of the
glory of their ancestors," a typical Caesarian irony, and
a bitter pill to the ruling class, for he imposed a democratic
constitution.[78] The weathercock Delians promptly erected
a statue to him as savior and benefactor; the superintendent of the island that year was Agathostratos son of
Dionysios of Pallene, a Keryx.[79] The Athenian demos followed suit.[80] An eyewitness writing to Cicero in 45 de-
scribes a scene of devastation: "Post me erat Aegina, ante
me Megara, dextra Piraeus, sinistra Corinthus: quae oppida
quodam tempore florentissima fuerant, nunc prostrata et
diruta ante oculos iacent."[81] But in that very year Caesar
rebuilt Corinth, and that spelled the end of the prosperity
of Delos and of those Athenian gennetai who derived income therefrom. Perhaps this is why the gennetai embraced
the cause of Brutus and Cassius: a Delian dedication to
Brutus and Cassius compares them to those eupatrid tyrant
slayers Harmodios and Aristogeiton;[82] another Delian
dedication honors Brutus' uncle, Quintus Hortensius—the
relationship is specified.[83] The Athenians—Areiopagos,
Boule, and demos—honored the memory of Caesar's enemy
Marcus Claudius Marcellus (cos. 51), who was murdered
by Caesarians in the Peiraieus, but cremated in the Academy, and his ashes placed in a marble tomb.[84]

Then Philippi doomed Brutus and Cassius—Cassius committed suicide in Athens. When the victors, Antony and
Octavian, fell out, Athens sided with Antony. The demos
made a dedication to his legate Marcus Cocceius Balbus, the
Areiopagos to his governor of Achaia, Lucius Marcius

Censorinus, who had given Aigina to Athens.[85] In an ephebe list of about 40 B.C., remarkable for the number of Roman names, eupatrids head the contingent of their tribes;[86] in an ephebe decree of 39/8–38/7, Antony is hailed as the New Dionysos.[87] In the Stoa of Attalos in Athens the Boeotians set up a dedication to Antony's proquaestor.[88] Meanwhile the gene maintained their connections with Delphi, as an exchange of letters (37/6) of the Gephyraioi and the Delphians shows.[89]

But Athens had again backed a lost cause. Antony was beaten at Actium, and in due course the adulation of the victor began. We find a dedication to Octavian on Delos,[90] in Athens one to the physician who had saved his life at Philippi by a timely warning.[91] The last stage of this eventful history is marked by the construction, to the east of the Parthenon, of the round temple of Rome and Augustus. The inscription on its epistyle survives: it is dated by reference to a hoplite-general and a priestess of Athena Polias, eupatrids.[92]

Conclusion

This is the appropriate place to end our story. The role of the Athenian aristocracy was not played out with the advent of Augustus, but a competent pen has recounted how the gennetai's deep roots, their will to endure, their sense of continuity enabled them to survive and to contribute to the Athenian Renaissance which we call the Second Sophistic.[93] Athens under Augustus produced no creative artists to rival those of Rome's Golden Age; nonetheless the Ara Pacis was carved by Athenian sculptors, and Vergil and Horace did acknowledge their debt to Athens.

Athenian aristocrats had been living sophisticated lives when Rome was still a village of mud huts on the Palatine Hill. Rome's rule of law looked back to Solon and Perikles; Rome's great builders followed in the tradition of Peisistratos. Rome was the poorer for not having produced a reformer like Kleisthenes; her empire would have been more popular if aristocrats like Kimon and Perikles, and not plutocrats, had administered it. Coriolanus lacked the flair of Alkibiades; Cicero acknowledged his inferiority to Demosthenes; compared to Lykourgos, Cato the Elder is a peasant. When Rome became the dominant power in the Mediterranean, she went to school at Athens. Even in decline, Athens' prestige still impressed Romans. Let Cicero have the last word: ''Adsunt Athenienses, unde humanitas, doctrina, religio, fruges, iura, leges ortae atque in omnes terras distributae putantur; de quorum urbis possessione propter pulchritudinem etiam inter deos certamen fuisse proditum est; quae vetustate ea est ut ipsa ex sese suos cives genuisse dicatur et eorum eadem terra parens, altrix, patria dicatur, auctoritate autem tanta est ut iam fractum prope ac debilitatum Graeciae nomen huius urbis laude nitatur.'' [94]

Notes

Chapter One: *From the Cup of Hemlock to the Poisoned Pen (399–322)*

1. Lys. 19.55. Yet this same man's father equipped triremes seven times (sec. 57).

2. [Dem.] 58.65 (339/8).

3. Isok. 19.36 puts the ideal into the mouth of a Siphnian.

4. Isae. 5.6.

5. Dem. 20.29.

6. On Proxenos: Dem. 19.230; J. Kirchner, *Prosopographia Attica,* 2 vols. (Berlin, 1901–1903; reprinted 1966) 12270 (hereafter *PA*); *IG* II² 5765 may be his gravestone; Demades *In Demosth.* 63; *Hesperia* 33 (1964) 226, no. 75. On Demokrates: *PA* 3521; Hypereides *In Philippidem* 2–3.

7. [Dem.] 49.6 and 22.

8. Dem. 20.115.

9. Dem. 21.182; cf. 24.135, where we find the Keryx Myronides in jail.

10. Lys. 27.10.

11. E.g. Dem. 3.21.

12. Dem. 54.34, and 9.

13. Dem. 27.52.

14. [Dem.] 48.55.

15. [Dem.] 58.40.

16. J. Sundwall, "Epigraphische Beiträge zur sozial-politischen Geschichte Athens im Zeitalter des Demosthenes," *Klio* Beiheft 4 (1906), a fundamental work. A revision by J. Davies of St. Andrews is announced.

17. Sundwall, 30.

18. 12.143.

19. Isok. 12.81 sees these qualities in Homeric heroes.

20. Isae. 11.

21. Dittenberger, *Sylloge Inscriptionum Graecarum* (hereafter *Syll.*³), 921; H. T. Wade-Gery, "Studies in the Structure of Attic Society: I. Demotionidai," *CQ* 25 (1931) 129–142. A. Andrewes ("Philochoros on Phratries," *JHS* 81 [1961] 1–15) calls them a genos outright.

22. [Andok.] 4 is almost entirely a personal attack, but it does mention how Alkibiades despises democracy (16), the awe in which he is held (18), the attempt to capitalize on the prestige of

Olympic victories (25), and the frequent ostracisms of Alkmaionids (34).

23. Isok. 16.25, and 31. Teisias may have been a member of the genos of Praxiergidai; see n. 31 below.

24. Lys. 14.18, 28, 39, 41–2.

25. Lys. 16.

26. W. R. M. Lamb, introduction to Loeb translation (London and New York 1930) 373.

27. *PA* 9674, with stemma.

28. Lys. 16.18.

29. *PA* 7826.

30. Andok. 1.

31. *Hesperia* 7 (1938) 92, no. 12. See further *PA* 7737. Improved stemma: *Polemon* 5 (1954) 144.

32. Lys. 19.48. The last known member of the family, Hipponikos son of Hipponikos of Alopeke (a town deme: see *Hesperia* 5 [1936] 400 no. 10 line 110), made a dedication to Iakchos in the third century (²4680). Is it more than coincidence that another Keryx, Aristeides' grandson, made a living as a dream interpreter at the shrine of Iakchos (Plut. *Arist.* 27)?

33. *PA* 3265, 3276, with stemma. We have not enough information to attach this stemma to that of Demosthenes, *PA* 1, pp. 242–243, but the connection may have been present to the mind of the author of *Vit. X Or* 844D, who gives the name of one of Demosthenes' guardians as Demophon *or* Demeas. On Demainetos as a fire-eater—like Demosthenes—see *Hellenika Oxyrhynchia, FGrHist* 66. Both families won athletic victories: *Syll.*³, 1074; *IG* II², 1138. On the allegations that Demosthenes' mother was a Scythian, A. Schaefer, *Demosthenes* I² (Berlin 1885) 268 compares the foreign mothers of the clansmen Kleisthenes, Themistokles, and Kimon. Demosthenes' wife's father, Heliodoros, was *eudokimos* (*Vit. X Or.* 847C). A Heliodoros of Bate was secretary of the genos of Amynandridai, *aet. Aug.* (*IG* II², 2338, line 11); an Ailios Heliodoros son of Athenodoros is recorded as a Keryx, *ca.* A.D. 200 (*ibid.* 2340 line 10); a Heliodoros son of Diodotos, from Demosthenes' deme, was *archon basileus* in 128/7 (Sundwall, *NPA* p. 88). Demosthenes' cousin Hippokleia was married to a Lykomid (*IG* II², 2670). The Bouzygai were priests of Zeus Teleios. Could the notorious *eteleis, ego d' eteloumen* of *De Cor.* 265 possibly be an oblique reference to this cult? Bouzygai legends connect the clan with Theseus' son Demophon (A. B. Cook, *Zeus* 3 [Cambridge 1940] 609); hence perhaps the name in Demosthenes' family. Should [Δημοφ]ῶν be restored in the inscription *BCH* 8.312?

34. Isae. 5, ed. W. Wyse (Cambridge 1904), stemma fac. p. 403.

35. Lys. 2. Genuineness supported by J. Walz, *Philologus* Supplbd. 29.4 (1936).

36. P. Shorey, *What Plato Said* (Chicago 1933) 6.

37. [Dem.] 60.

38. Hyp. 6.

39. Shorey, *What Plato Said*, 185–188. Genuineness supported by N. Scholl, *Der platonische Menexenus* (Rome 1959) and J. von Lowenclau, same title, *Tüb. Beitr.* (Stuttgart 1961).

40. Shorey, 187.

41. E.g. in *Helen* (10.47) he ascribes recognition of the advantages of noble breeding to Paris, whose usual role in Greek literature is that of villain.

42. Isok. 4.157.

43. *GHI* 2, no. 123.

44. *IG* II², 40. Wilhelm (*IG* II² Add. p. 657) read the mover as Kephalos (*PA* 8277) mover of the charter of the confederacy. But the traces on the stone make Stephanos the more likely restoration.

45. [Dem.] 59.10. Ann Pippin Burnett (*Historia* 11 [1962] 1–17) rejects the identification as making his career begin too early, and mentions as a possibility the Stephanos who was an arbitrator in the Salaminioi decree of 363/2 (below, n. 63).

46. *PA* 9972.

47. As implied by Kirchner, *PA* 9972. The card file of Attic names at the Institute for Advanced Study, Princeton, records 21 Menexenoi from 6 different demes. In Plato's dialogue *Menexenus* (234 B) an aristocrat, Archinos of Koile, is mentioned as delivering a funeral oration over those who fell in battle at Nemea (374).

48. C. W. J. Eliot, *Coastal Demes of Attica* (Toronto 1962) 99–104.

49. *IG* II², 3679, 3688.

50. *PA* 13700.

51. 15.101–139, esp. 138.

52. His son bore the Bouzyges name Demostratos. See *PA* 3617, 3611. On his role in politics, see R. Sealey, "Athens after the Social War," *JHS* 75 (1955) 74–81. On Aristogeiton: id., *BICS London* 7 (1960) 33–43.

53. Konon III was Peiraieus general in 333/2 (*AM* 76 [1961] 143 n. 2). The Athenians repented of their harshness to his father: a monument to him was found in the Agora (*Hesperia* 30 [1961] 267 no. 89).

54. *Rep.* 548A–549.

55. *Laws* 741 B–C. On the late date of alienation of property: J. V. A. Fine, "Horoi," *Hesperia* Suppl. 9 (1951) 167–208.

56. *Rep.* 474 D. Cf. Thouk. 3.82.

57. J. Beloch, *Attische Politik seit Perikles* (Leipzig 1884) 167.

58. M. Crosby, "The Leases of the Laureion Mines," *Hesperia* 19 (1950) 189–312; *ibid.* "More Fragments of the Mining Leases from the Athenian Agora"; *idem* 26 (1957) 1–23; S. Lauffer, "Prosopographische Bemerkungen zu den attischen Grubenpachtlisten," *Historia* 6 (1957) 287–305; R. J. Hopper, "The Attic Silver Mines in the Fourth Century," *BSA* 48 (1953) 200–254.

59. *PA* 9395.

60. *PA* 9667, 9676.

61. *PA* 11950.

62. *Hesperia* 19 (1950) 235, no. 13, line 67; *ibid.* 7 (1938) 3 no. 1, line 69.

63. W. S. Ferguson, "The Salaminioi of Heptaphylai and Sounion," *Hesperia* 7 (1938) 24. Text conveniently reprinted in *SEG* 21 (1965) 193–198, no. 527. See also D. D. Feaver, "Historical Development in the Priesthoods of Athens," *YCS* 15 (1957) 123–158, esp. 128–130.

64. Stemma by B. D. Meritt, *Hesperia* 26 (1957) 43. The father of Plato's Theaitetos, Euphronios, is described as *eudokimos* (144C) and is from Sounion. Might he be a Salaminios?

65. If the priestess on her marriage to a gennetes retained her prerogatives and passed them on to her daughter, the possibility is created of a person's apparently belonging to more than one genos. The same applies to the Eteoboutad priestess of Athena Polias. Such cases become more common in Hellenistic and Roman Athens.

66. Published by G. Daux, *BCH* 87 (1963) 603–634; interpretation by S. Dow, *ibid.* 89 (1965) 180–213, esp. 210.

67. Beloch, *Attische Politik*, 171.

68. *IG* II², 123 (Hegesandros); *ibid.* 125 (Hegesippos).

69. *PA* 6307.

70. *PA* 11925, 11950.

71. *IG* II², 2338, line 44.

72. Plut. *Phocion* 9.9.

73. Isok. 7.

74. F. Jacoby, *FGrHist* IIIb, Suppl. 1 (Leiden 1954) 112.

75. Beloch, *Attische Politik*, 174.

76. Philochoros, *FGrHist*, IIIb, No. 328, F 155; *Syll.³*, 204 and Kirchner's note there, p. 279. Jacoby draws attention to a Thrasyphon s. of Hierekleides who moved honorary decrees for Eleusinian cult officials *ca.* 275/4 (²683, 1235). On the date, see chap. ii, n. 45.

77. Dem. 14.41.

78. Shorey, *What Plato Said*, 42; Plato, *Ep.* 7,324 B–326 B.

79. *Laws*, 365. On aristocratic elements in the *Laws*, see Glenn R. Morrow, *Plato's Cretan City* (Princeton 1960) 229–233, 530.

80. Shorey, *What Plato Said*, 356.

81. Frequencies: Hellenes, 65 times: polis, 59; polemos, 54; pratto, 49; basileus, 31; barbaros, 31; dynamis, 27; tyche, 25; archo, 19; peitho, 18; kaka, 17; strateia, 16; apallaxis, 15.

82. Frequencies: Philippos, 22 times; eirene, 20; psephisma, 19; chora, 14; dikaios, 12; presbeis, 11; ktaomai and epanorthosis, 9 each; adikos and homologeo, 8 each; euergetema, thalatta, Hellenes and symbolon, 7 each; diaballo, diadikazo, 6 each; allotrios, lambano, dorea, nomos, polis, phylatto, 5 each; symmachia, katapseudomai, 4 each.

83. Ed. E. Bikerman and J. Sykutris, *SB Lpz* 80.3 (1928). Note that Speusippos' patronymic contains the root of his genos name, Medontidai. Word analysis suggests doubt about the authenticity of the letter.

84. [Dem.] 59.61. The seven gennetai come from six widely scattered demes. Ferguson (*Hesperia* 7 [1938] 23) uses other similar examples to argue for the artificiality of gene, in which, he claims, kinship is a fiction.

85. *IG* II², 373, line 20.

86. *Ibid.* 1927, lines 76–77.

87. *Ibid.* 1251, 1632 line 280.

88. Dem. 8.

89. Dem. 9.

90. As argued by the Loeb editors, N. J. and N. W. DeWitt. See also A. Lesky, *Geschichte der griechischen Literatur*² (Bern 1963) 652 (Eng. translation [1966] 605) with literature cited there.

91. *IG* II², 237.

92. *Ibid.* 291.

93. Philokles of Phrearria, *Hesperia* 30 (1961) 33 line 215, and p. 47.

94. *Hesperia* 21 (1952) 355–356 no. 5; M. Ostwald, "The Athenian Legislation against Tyranny and Subversion," *TAPA* 86 (1955) 103–128.

95. [Plut.] *Vit. X. Or.* in *Mor.* 841B–844A.

96. 842D.

97. *IG* II², 1628 line 280 (355/4); *ibid.* 1672, lines 11, 302 (329/8); *Vita X Or.* 844A: honors to Diotimos, to whom he sent reinforcements. Diotimos may be the general mentioned in *IG* II², 414 fg. a; see Schweigert's restoration, *Hesperia* 9 (1940) 340–341.

98. *Ibid.* 457 (the honors proposed by Stratokles in 307/6); 351 (Lykourgos moves honors to a Plataean who contributed to his building projects).

99. H. A. Thompson and R. L. Scranton, "Stoas and City Walls on the Pnyx," *Hesperia* 12 (1943) 269–383.

100. The longest is from Euripides' *Erechtheus*. A new papyrus (*Recherches de Papyrologie* 4) contains part of 120 lines from the end of this play, which give something close to a foundation-charter for the Eteoboutadai and explain their claim to the priest-hood of Athena Polias.

101. *Vit. X. Or.* 842A, C, F; 841F.

102. *IG* II², 333 (*leges sacrae*); 337 (a temenos for Aphrodite of Kition); *Syll.³*, 298 (Oropos); *ibid.* 296 (Delphi).

103. *Vit. X Or.* 843E; Paus. 1.26.5.

104. *IG* II², 3207 (crowns), belongs with 457, as Wilhelm showed in 1925 (*Attische Urkunden* 3.1–6).

105. *Vit. X. Or* 843B–C.

106. *Ibid.* 841B–C; *IG* II², 1191 (Xenokles superintendent of mysteries); the bridge was the subject of an epigram: *Anth. Pal.* 9.147; *IG* II², 1628 lines 400, 414–415; *Hesperia* 10 (1941) 42 no. 10; *ibid.* 29 (1960) 2 no. 3 (*ca.* 330); *PA* 11234: a great grandson was a contributor in 232/1.

107. *Ath. Pol.* 54.6–7.

108. F. Jacoby, *FGrHist* IIIb Suppl. 1 (Leiden 1954) pp. 57–255.

109. Ammonios of Anaphlystos, a descendant of Philochoros, places the daidouchos' two torches as a symbol on his coins; he was first mint-magistrate in 150/49 (M. Thompson, *The New Style Silver Coinage of Athens* [New York 1961] 549–550.) See the stemma in P. Roussel, *Délos, colonie athénienne* (Paris 1914) 104. An attempt by D. M. Lewis (*NC* 5.7.2 [1962] 275–300) to lower Miss Thompson's dates by 33 years does not appear to fit the prosopographical evidence.

110. Jacoby, *FGrHist*, 96. *Syll.³*, 193 contains the warm praise of Androtion by the Arkesinoi (357/6). See *PA* 915; Androtion's father Andron (*PA* 921) was a member of the 400 and the accuser of Antiphon. On Androtion as a faction leader, see R. Sealey, "Athens after the Social War," *JHS* 75 (1955) 74–81. Demosthenes' second cousin Demon II (stemma *PA* 3595) may be the author of the *Atthis, On Sacrifices,* and *On Proverbs,* cited *FGrHist* 3B, No. 327.

111. Jacoby, *FGrHist* 100. Phanodemos served as councillor or arbitrator in 330/29; *IG* II², 1924, 2409, 2397, 2423 (joined by D. M. Lewis, *BSA* 50 (1955) 27–36; *Syll.³*, 296, 298.

112. D. M. Lewis, *BSA* 50 (1955) 35.

113. *ArchEph* 1917, 41.

114. *IG* II², 1629, line 18.

115. *Ibid.*, 1750 lines 7, 25.

116. Jacoby, *FGrHist* 227, 223.

117. *Ibid.* 224.

118. *Ath. Pol.* 42; Chr. Pelekidis, *L'histoire de l'ephébie attique* (Paris 1962) 83–86; Plato, *Laws.* 762B.

119. Aischines' claim (2.147) that his family "shared the same altar as the Eteoboutadai" tells us more about his pretensions than about his pedigree.

120. W. W. Goodwin (ed.), *Demosthenes on the Crown* (Cambridge 1901) 328–329.

121. Dem. 18, *On the Crown.*

122. *Ibid.* 208.

123. *History of Greece* 10.299.

124. *Hesperia* 8 (1939) 27–30, no. 7.

125. *Vit. X. Or* (Demosthenes) 846C.

126. A. W. Pickard-Cambridge, *Demosthenes* (New York 1914) 479.

Chapter Two: *The Gene in the Hellenistic Age (322–166 B.C.)*

1. W. S. Ferguson, *Hellenistic Athens* (hereafter *HA*) (London 1911) 24–25. Mention of the Solonian constitution calls to mind an honorific decree of Solon's (and Plato's) genos, the Medontidai (*IG* II², 1233), dated sometime in the fourth century. The dates in this chapter are those of B. D. Meritt, *The Athenian Year* (Berkeley 1961), esp. pp. 231–238.

2. S. Dow, "Athenians Real, Dubious, and Non-existent," *Studies Presented to D. M. Robinson* 2 (St. Louis 1953) 362; cf. *IG* II², 896 and 2332. References below will omit '*IG* II.'

3. *PA* 5217 (stemma): Toepffer, *Attische Genealogie* (Berlin, 1889) 133; ²3845 (statue).

4. ²1191; PA 11234; *SEG* 19. no. 119. See above chap. i n. 106. ²2840 is a dedication by Xenokles to Demeter and Korê. In 307/6 he was *agonothetes*; the comic poet Philemon was one of the contestants (²3073, cf. 3077).

5. *HA* 92–3 is especially evocative. For the date of the *Characters*, see the Jebb-Sandys edition (Cambridge 1909) 5.

6. *PA* 3455, which gives the references. The most up-to-date

collection of testimonies and fragments is F. Wehrli's, *Die Schule des Aristoteles* 4 (Basel 1949). See also *FGrHist* no. 228.

7. Vitruvius *de arch.* 7, *praef.* 17.

8. *HA* 73–94, a brilliant exploitation of New Comedy as sociological document.

9. E. W. Handley, *The Dyskolos of Menander* (London 1965) 9.

10. U. von Wilamowitz-Moellendorff, *Griech. Literatur* (Berlin 1905), 130.

11. Stemma, *PA* 5547.

12. Plut. *Demetrios* 23, 24, 26. Yet statues of Demetrios and his father were erected beside those of the tyrant-slaying Gephyraioi, Harmodios and Aristogeiton.

13. For the suggestion that the figure of Demea in Terence's *Adelphoe* (adapted from Menander) may be a parody of Stratokles, while the urbane Micio represents Demetrios of Phaleron, see my "Demetrius of Phalerum, Cato, and the *Adelphoe*," *Athenaeum n.s.* 32 (1954) 18–35.

14. See above, chap. i n. 98. ²3776 is the base of a statue of Lykourgos of about this date. See also ²4259, another statue base, perhaps of Augustan date.

15. ²643 and 1492; *PA* 15, [Plut.] *Vit. X Or.* 843 A.

16. ²3455 and 776 (with stemma) ; *PA* 9615.

17. Pind. *Nem.* 2.25. Toepffer *Attische Genealogie* 313 is equivocal.

18. ²1487, line 79. Demochares wrote a history of his own times: *FGrHist* 2A, no. 75.

19. *PA* 3716.

20. D. L. 10.1; *PA* 4855.

21. *Hesperia* 1 (1932) 45 fig. 13.

22. ²2501.

23. ²1232.

24. *Hesperia* 9 (1940) 104–105 no. 20.

25. ²2944, 1230; *Hesperia* 8 (1939) 177–180 = ²1194, 1274, new fragment; 1231; 2976 (an ephebe descendant of Konon); 1363. The mover of ²1230, a decree of the genos, is himself a Keryx (cf. ²2812 and ²6587), as noted by D. M. Lewis, *BSA* 50 (1955) 17. If the family of Euthydemos (stemma *Hesperia* 8 [1939] 180) is Keryx, it is unique in having an Eleusinian demotic. It was in any case prominent in religion, local and international politics, and war, as the stemma shows. ²1363 has been reedited by S. Dow and R. F. Healey (*Harv. Theol. Stud.* 21 [1965]) who see in it (it is an Eleusinian religious calendar) another example (see above, chap. i n. 66) from between 330 and

270 B.C., of non-gennetai taking over gentile prerogatives. But the Eumolpids and Kerykes are still indispensable to the rites, and the recipients of a fine meal at public expense.

26. *PA* 6165. See note 65 below.

27. ²649; new text, W. B. Dinsmoor, *Archons of Athens* (Cambridge 1932) 7. The date is Meritt's, *Ath. Yr.* 232.

28. 289/8 (²682); 288/7 (*ibid.* 650, 651); 287/6 (*ibid.* 653, 655); 282/1 (*ibid.* 670).

29. *HA* 165–167.

30. S. Dow, "Prytaneis" *Hesperia* Suppl. 1 (1937).

31. R. Schlaifer, "Notes on Athenian Public Cults," *HSCP* 51 (1940) 233–260, criticized by W. K. Pritchett, "A Note on Epigraphic Methodology," *Hesperia* 10 (1941) 396–397.

32. E.g. ²678 (256/5 [Meritt]). On Eukles' family see *Hesperia* 3 (1934) 27 no. 19, and 26 (1957) 41–42; on the possibility that heralds of the Boule and demos might belong to the genos of Kerykes, W. Dittenberger, *Hermes* 20 (1885) 37.

33. ²1235. But Meritt notes: "characteristic letters of the period 230 B.C."

34. [Plut.] *Vit. X Or.* 851D; *HA* 172–173.

35. ²682, *Syll.*³, 409. *PA* 13963; 13964 (stemma). There is a good article on Phaidros by K. J. Beloch, *RFIC* 51 (1923) 273–286.

36. ²687; see above, n. 3.

37. *HA* 176–183. The Ptolemaic fort at Koroni on the east coast of Attika, published by E. Vanderpool, J. R. McCredie, and Arthur Steinberg (*Hesperia* 31 [1962] 26–61), obviously proved inadequate to change the course of the war. The original excavators have refused (*ibid.* 33 [1964] 69–75) to accept the earlier dating proposed by G. Roger Edwards (*ibid.* 32 [1963] 109–111) on grounds of pottery, and Virginia Grace (*ibid.* 319–334) on grounds of amphoras. See now J. R. McCredie, "Fortified Military Camps in Attica." *Hesperia Suppl.* 9 (1966).

38. ²782. The decree is fragmentary, but since it mentions an *architekton* it had something to do with building. Meritt dates it 250/49. The same man was elected proxenos of the Boeotians at Oropos (*Eph. Arch.* [1919] 75 no. 106).

39. ²2434; *PA* 6306.

40. ²791d line 32; *ibid.* 847 line 44; *cf. ibid.* 3857 (from Eleusis). For the genos, *ibid.* 1136; stemma, *PA* 10759. From midcentury comes a possible gennetes, Aristonymos Pitheus (Kekropis) who served Erechtheis as priest (*Hesperia* 33 [1964] 171–173 no. 26).

41. ²4676, ²12917 (part of same stele, with the name Philia);

HA 241; Polyb. 5.106.6ff. Stemma *PA* 5966. Later, when it became politic, the priesthood was linked with the goddess Roma. Mikion III may have sat in the theater of Dionysos between the priest of Democracy and the priest of Ptolemy III and Berenike: A. E. Raubitschek, "Demokratia," *Akte des IV . . . Kongresses für . . . Epigraphik* (Vienna 1964) 332–337, esp. 336.

42. ²1245 (249/8 [Meritt]); *HA* 204 ff.

43. In ²1245 he is archon of the Mesogeioi; Schlaifer's attempt (*CP* 39 [1944] 22–27) to make them a genos depends on a restoration.

44. ²3474; *HA* 201.

45. ²683; *ibid.* 1235; see chap. i n. 76. He also appears in ²787 (236/5), see S. Dow, *AJA* 40 (1936) 62. But the archon of 221/0 had a different demotic: *Hesperia* 23 (1954) 244 no. 17.

46. ²791; new text: *Hesperia* 11 (1942) 287 no. 56.

47. ²1705.

48. ²1300.

49. *HA* 232–234.

50. *HA* 206–207.

51. ²834.

52. ²859; *HA* 208.

53. ²1706.

54. Paraphrased *HA* 261–263.

55. Attalos was initiated into the Mysteries in 199 (Livy 31.47).

56. *HA* 275–276, movingly eloquent pages.

57. *HA* 256 with n. 2. The date, however, is Meritt's, for the archon Dionysios, in whose year Eurykleides' son Mikion had already succeeded to the priesthood of Demos and Graces (²2798).

58. *HA* 277.

59. *HA* chap. VII.

60. *HA* 282, 288.

61. M. Thompson, *New Style Coinage,* chap. 6 n. 109, from whom the dates and prosopographical detail in what follows are taken.

62. E. A. Sydenham, *Coinage of the Roman Republic* (London 1952); A. Alföldi, "The Main Aspects of Political Propaganda on the Coins of the Roman Republic," *Essays in Roman Coinage presented to H. Mattingly* (Oxford 1956) 63–95. Examples: the flamen's cap, which may be a pun on Flamininus; Venus Genetrix, patron of his gens, on the coins of Sex. Julius Caesar.

63. The best evidence is the daidouchos' torches chosen as symbol by the Ammonios who was first mint-magistrate in 150/49. But the *kerchnos* on the 182/1 series is an Eleusinian symbol.

64. Adeimantos' symbol is the trident, a clear reference to Posei-

don. If to Poseidon Erechtheus, he is Eteoboutad; if to Phytal-
mios, he belongs to the Phytalidai (*AG* 252, 254). On Adeimantos
as priest of the eponymos in 173/2, see below, n. 72.

65. Echedemos' symbol is Helios. An epigram (*Anth. Pal.*
12.55) refers to him as a second Apollo; an inscription of a later
Echedemos (²3900, "fin.s.i.a.") bears a tripod in a monogram form
(cf. ²575) which may be resolved into *PYTHIOU*. Apollo Pythios
was the patron of the Kephalidai (*AG* 265).

66. *HA* 287 and n. 4. Not only names but symbols. On these on
the "Wappenmünzen" of 6th-century Athens, see C. T. Seltman,
Athens, its History and Coinage (Cambridge 1924).

67. Livy 37.7.

68. Plut. *Cato* 12; *HA* 283.

69. *Hesperia* 26 (1957) 32 no. 5, which is said to be by the same
hand as *ibid.* 17 (1948) 17 no. 8, a decree of Erechtheis.

70. Dow, *Pryt.* 120 no. 64.

71. *Hesperia* 33 (1964) 191 no. 40. Stemma: Dow, *Pryt.* 123.

72. *Hesperia* 26 (1957) 33 no. 6.

73. See especially ²902 (=*Pryt.* 111 no. 55) of 182/1.

74. Head, *HN*¹ 325.

75. ²785 with Kirchner's notes.

76. ²2332 with Kirchner's notes.

77. ²2314.

78. ²2331.

79. ²4931a.

80. *PA* 8252; Thompson, *New Style Coinage,* 158–160. Miss
Thompson does not identify this Antiochos with Antiochos V, but
grants that the elephant symbol must be a tribute to the Seleucids.

81. *HA* 315, 321–322.

Chapter Three: *From the Reacquisition of Delos to the Battle of
Actium (166–31)*

1. On Roman Athens, besides Ferguson, see J. Day, *An Economic History of Athens under Roman Domination* (N.Y. 1942)
50–133; and S. Accame, *Il dominio romano in Grecia* (Rome 1946)
163–187.

2. M. Thompson, *New Style Coinage,* 546ff.

3. P. Roussel, *Mélanges Bidez* 2 (Paris 1934) 819–834. Stemma
IG II², 3510. See n. 46 below. The date is probably 21/0: see O.

Reinmuth, "The Attic Archons Named Apolexis," *BCH* 90 (1966) 93–100.

4. Stemma *PA* 2, p. 82; for the Eteoboutad connection, see the stemma, *ibid.* 1, 22. Four generations later, a descendant of Lysandros and Glaukos married into the family which is the subject of the *Mélanges Bidez* decree.

5. *PA* 5965, 10187.

6. For the priesthood, see now *Hesperia* 26 (1957) 343 no. 27. Miss Thompson thinks Ariarathes is not the prince of Cappadocia, but only named in his honor. But see *Fouilles de Delphes* (hereafter *FdD*) III, 2.12; *Inscriptions de Délos* (hereafter *IdD*) 1827–9; *Hesperia* 17 (1948) 25, no. 12.

7. A descendant, Aristaichmos, son of Ammonios of Anaphlystos, appears on the *Mélanges Bidez* decree. Kallias was a well-known Keryx name in the fifth century.

8. *PA* 6651.

9. For a descendant of Sokrates, priest of Delian Apollo, see *IdD* 1936, 1835. For connections with Eurykleides and Mikion, see *PA* 13089–13090: Sokrates third magistrate on their coins. A Dionysiodoros appears in the *Mélanges Bidez* decree.

10. The rare name Eumareides occurs at Delphi (*FdD* III 2.21) as ephebe escort to the Pythais of 138, and in Athens (^{2}2980) as a victor in a torch race. A Kleomenes is lithophoros in *MB* 18; the lithophoros had a seat reserved for him in the Theater of Dionysos: ^{2}5077. The name is rare; only six entries in *PA*.

11. Protagoras: ^{2}950 (new text: *Hesperia* 28 [1959] 185, no. 7); Chrysis: ^{2}1136, ^{2}3484–6. Stemma: *PA* 10759.

12. ^{2}3474; see also ^{2}3473, ^{2}3870.

13. ^{2}3477. Stemma, *PA* 5966.

14. Stemma: *PA* ^{2}2332$_{189-193}$; ^{2}2864; ^{2}1937$_9$.

15. ^{2}957$_{41}$; ^{2}2334$_{71-73}$.

16. ^{2}956II$_{72}$; ^{2}957II$_{31-32,\,64}$.

17. *Hermes* 28 (1893), 620 = *FdD* III 2.13.

18. ^{2}1036$_{43}$.

19. *SEG* 19, no. 124; see *Hesperia* 11 (1942) 293, no. 58. Aristokles' name should be restored as hierophant in ^{2}1045$_5$ and its date changed to mid-century. Amynomachos as hierophant: ^{2}3469, following Meritt in lowering Kirchner's date.

20. ^{2}1236 with Kirchner's note; *HA* 261, n. 1.

21. ^{2}2317$_{37,47,48}$.

22. ^{2}1938$_{25,57}$. For the Eteoboutad connection see stemma, *PA* 1, p. 22, for the Eumolpid, *ibid.* 2, p. 82 (Medeios IV: ^{2}3490).

23. ^{2}2358$_{22}$. On the Salaminioi of Sounion see *Hesperia* 7 (1938) 24; *SEG* 21 (1965) 193–198, no. 527.

24. *HA* 354–355; *BCH* 32 (1908) 306–368 (a prosopography of Delos), nos. 94, 251, 252, 255, 261, 264, 423; M. Thompson, *New Style Coinage,* 28.

25. *IdD* 2589; ²1939–1940. ²2445 (*ca.* 140), a list of unknown purpose, contains, out of 17 names, one certain Keryx, Demeas son of Demeas of Halai (guaranteed by the *Mélanges Bidez* inscription), and one man, Mantias of Marathon, who married into a family possibly of the Salaminian genos, that of Dositheos of Myrrhinoutta (²3488, with stemma: Mantias' daughter is *arrephoros* [peplos-weaver; she appears as *ergastine,* ²1034; see below, n. 47] to Athena Polias and Pandrosos: the priestess of Pandrosos came from the Salaminioi). The relation between *arrephoroi* and *ergastinai* is missed by W. Burkert, "Kekropidensage und Arrephoria," *Hermes* 94 (1966) 5 n. 3, 22 n. 4. The *arrephoros* Xenostrate of ²3473 (*ca.* 150) has a like-named *ergastine* grandniece (²1036$_{37}$).

26. *Hesperia* 21 (1952) 359 no. 7 52–53 = *SEG* 12 (1955) no. 101; see chap. ii, nn. 70 and 71; *Hesperia* 32 (1963) 21 no. 21.

27. *HA* 370–3; *FdD* III 2.47–49; the decree of 129/8 is most conveniently accessible in *SEG* 21 (1965) 159 no. 469.

28. ²2452.

29. P. Roussel, *Délos,* 100. Medeios (II): stemma *PA* 2, p. 82, *FdD* III 2.12.2$_4$; *IdD* 1869; *FdD* III 2.28IV$_{52}$, ²1713, ²2459$_{1.6}$, ²2336 (in ed. by S. Dow, *HSCP* 51 [1940] 117–124), lines 94, 167, 185, 187, 191; *IdD* 1711, 1757, 1761, 1816, 2400; M. Thompson, *New Style Coinage,* index, s. v. Medeios; [Plut.] *Vit. X. Or.* 843B; *Hesperia* 33 (1964) 193 no. 43 (honored by prytany, along with Oinophilos of Aphidna [see below, n. 71]). Sarapion: ²2452$_{33}$, *FdD* III 2.28$_{45}$, Dow, lines 50, 228, 143, 208, 210, 212, 214; *FdD* III, 2.6.54; *IdD* 2005, ²3881. On these inscriptions he is recorded as member of the Pythais of 106/5, honored as founder, and chief of the Pythais of 97/6, epimeletes of Delos, agonothetes of four festivals (Eleusinia, Dionysia, Panathenaia, Delia), recipient of statues. The elegiacs on Aropos: *BCH* 16 (1892) 150, no. 1. Dionysios and Nikon of Pallene: *PA* 4237, *NPA* 61. Demeas of Halai: *IdD* 2045. A full discussion of the Delphian Pythais is to be found in G. Daux, *Delphes au IIe et au Ier Siècle* (Paris 1936) 521–583.

30. M. Thompson, *New Style Coinage,* 587–599. I append a tabular view (M = mint-magistrate) on pages 81 and 82.

31. Demochares son of Menander of Azenia is third of twenty petitioners to honor Theophrastos of the *Mélanges Bidez* inscription. The family of Argeios of Trikorynthos is specifically mentioned as Keryx in an inscription of the Pythais of 106/5 (*FdD* III 2.13 II$_{11}$). Menedemos of Kydathenaion had a de-

Date	M1 Aropos	M2 Mnesagoras	Genos Eumolpid-Eteoboutad	Symbol
128/7				winged *agôn* (agonothetes in family of Medeios)
127/6	Xenokles	Harmoxenos	M1 Keryx (daidouchos)	coiled serpent
126/5	Nikogenes	Kallimachos	M2 Keryx	Hermes
125/4	Demeas	Hermokles	M1 prob. Keryx	Isis headdress
124/3	Xenokles	Harmoxenos	M1 Keryx	dolphin and trident
123/2	"	"	"	Roma
121/0	Apellikon	Gorgias	"	griffin
118/7	Mentor	Moschion	Gephyraioi	Harmodios and Aristogeiton
117/6	Architimos	Demetrios	M1 prob. Keryx	Isis
116/5	Lysandros	Oinophilos	M2 Philleidai	poppy-head, grain-ears
115/4	Amphias	"	Philleidai, father and son	Demeter
112/1	Sotades	Themistokles	M2 Keryx	bakchos
109/8	Theophrastos	"	Kerykes	looped fillet, or possibly cables
107/6	Demeas	Kallikratides	Keryx, Eumolpid	Isis
103/2	Menedemos	Timokrates	M1 Philleidai	Demeter
102/1	Menneas	Herodes	M1 Keryx	Hekate
101/0	Dionysios	Demostratos	Kerykes, father and son	winged caduceus
100/99	Demochares	Pammenes	M1 Keryx; M2 Erysichthonid-Keryx-Gephyraios	cicada
99/8	Diokles	Leonides	M2 Keryx	Asklepios
98/7	Philokrates	Herodes	M2 Keryx	Dionysos
97/6	Kallimachos	Epikrates	Kerykes, prob. father and son	Triptolemos
96/5	Architimos	Pammenes	M1 prob. Keryx; M2, see 100/99	filleted thyrsos

Date	M1	M2	Genos	Symbol
95/4	Diokles II	Medeios	M2 Eumolpid-Eteoboutad; brothers-in-law	Hygieia
94/3	Apellikon	Aristoteles	Kerykes, brothers	Demeter
92/1	Philokrates	Kalliphon	M1 Keryx	Nike
91/0	Tryphon	Polycharmos	M1 prob. Keryx (Herald of Areiopagos)	Hekate
89/8	Diokles	Medeios	M2: see 95/4; brothers-in-law	Athena Parthenos (M1's wife priestess of Athena)
88/7	Apolexis	Lysandros	Kerykes, father and son	Artemis

scendant who was priestess of Demeter and Kore (²3475, 4690). Hipparchos (119/8) and Kallias (94/3) bear Peisistratid and Keryx names respectively, but the latter may be of Bate; the name is very common. Sarapion (116/5) may have been of Melite, and therefore related to Medeios. Philanthes (87/6) may be of the family from Phyle one of whose daughters was priestess of Demeter and Kore (²3495, ca. 68; stemma, PA 11339).

32. BCH 30 (1906) 184; HA 429 n. 2. Later references: a Eumolpid in 56/5 (²1717); Kerykes in the reign of Augustus and after: ²1720–22, 1736. But Meritt would date 1720 "ca. 50 B.C."

33. Orosius 5.9.

34. HSCP 51 (1940) 117–124, lines 6, 50, 168, 208.

35. O. Reinmuth, Hesperia 24 (1955) 220–239 = SEG 15 (1958) no. 104. For an ephebe reading-list (mostly lost plays) see ²2363.

36. ²2452. Eumolpids: Lakrateides II son of Sostratos of Ikaria (line 41), Hierophantes son of Theophemos of Kydathenaion (48), Hierophantes son of Eustrophos of the Peiraieus (53), Hierophantes son of Menekleides of Kydathenaion (59). Kerykes: Mnesitheos son of Mnesitheos of Kydathenaion (6); Diodoros son of Theophilos of Halai (56), Xenokles son of Apollodoros of Otryne (4). Eteoboutadai: Mikion IV and Eurykleides III, sons of Eurykleides II, and Eurykleides IV son of Mikion IV, all of Kephisia (2, 5, 58). Philleidai: Asklepiades son of Xenon of Phlya (24), Menedemos son of Archon of Kydathenaion (30). Philaidai: Ophelas son of Miltiades, Miltiades son of Ophelas, both of the family deme of Lakiadai (13, 14). Medeios (28), Aropos (55), Sarapion (33).

37. ²2949: Pistokrates and Apollodoros, sons of Satyros of Auridai. Their grandfather Satyros: ²2332₇₈.

38. FdD III 2.13: Nikias son of Philoxenos. His son: ²2360₄.

39. ²2871, Theodosios son of Dios of Lakiadai, "of the mystic house of the genos of [Kyn]neidai." He may have been archon in 100/99: ²2336 = Dow, HSCP 51 (1940) 120, line 139.

40. Syll.³, 704 (Delphi) = ²1134, tr. Ferguson, HA 308–9.

41. Cic., de or. 1.82.

42. HA 428.

43. ²1013, its complex contents well summarized by Ferguson, HA 429–430. Diodoros' family as eupatrid: FdD, III 2.59–64; as Keryx: Mél. Bidez, line 20; as Gephyraios: Hesperia 9 (1940) 86 no. 17, which adds to and revises ²1096. Philonides, the archon of the genos, is from Paiania, not Aphidna, the seat of most known members of the genos.

44. ²2336, re-edited by Dow, HSCP 51 (1940) 116–124.

45. Details are shown on pp. 84–87.

Line	Name	Genos	Evidence	Post Held	Other Posts in Family	Remarks
6–7	Ammonios of Ana-phlystos	Keryx	*Mél. Bid.*$_{27}$ see note 46 below	Hopl.-gen'l	M1, M2, sup't Delos, HG, Pr. Apollo, arch., theoros	Descent from Philochoros
24	Demeas of Halai	? "	MB_{30} see note 46 below	Supt. Peir. harbor	Supt. Delos. Priestess of Demeter, M1	
28	Metrodoros of Kydathenaion	Eum.	$2242_{48,59}$ stemma, *PA* 9902	gymn., Delos	hierophant, treasurer, Her. Areiop., councillor, *kosmetes*	
42	Diophantos of Marathon	unspec.	Philochoros, *FGrHist* 328, F75	Pr. Hagn. Theou	*epi ta hiera*, Pr. Zeus Kynth, M1, Pr. Gt. Gods, envoy of tetrapolis	all envoys fr. Tetrapolis from one (unspecified) genos
50	Sarapion of Melite	Keryx	$MB_{21,22}$ see note 46 below	HG, agono-thetes	Supt. Delos, architheoros, HG, sub-priestess of Artemis	Gentile affiliation in collateral line

				Herald (Delos)		
93	Philon of Paiania	?Gephyraioi	*Hesperia* 9 (1940) 86 no. 17	Herald (Delos)	Sec'y to pryt.; thesmothetes	Philonides, archon of genos 37/6, Aeschines in stenma
96	Medeios of Peiraieus	Eteo., Eum.	[Plut.] *Vit.* X *Or.* 743B. ; 23490	archon, HG, agonothetes Supt. Delos, state bank	Pr. Poseidon Erechtheus, Eum. exegetes, Priestess of Ath. Polias, arch., trierarch, gymnasiarch	Desc. fr. orator Lykourgos; intermarriage with Kerykes
120	Dionysodoros of Deiradiotai	Keryx ?Erysichth.	$MB_{27,28}$ (corrected) see note 46 below	gymn., Delos	Pr. Amynos, arch., HA, councillor, thesmothetes, HG	Double adoption; gentile affiliation in Sounion line?
128	Asklepiades of Halai	Eteo.	23173	Pr. of Dionysos	poet; M1, M2, councillor	G. dau. priestess of Ath. Pol., Eteo. prerogative, Ephesian descent, Theban hon. citizenship

Line	Name	Genos	Evidence	Post Held	Other Posts in Family	Remarks
136	Theobios s. of Dionysios	?Amyn.	²2338; *FdD* III2, 48₂₀	Pr. Sarapis, Pr. Hagn. Theou	Pr. Zeus Kynth., Hellenotamias, trierarch, arch., councillor	Poss. connection w. Theophrastos, Agora-builder on Delos
147	Dionysios of Pallene	Keryx	MB_8	Supt. Peir. harbor	Supt. Delos, HG, councillor	
154	Theodosios of Lakiadai	?Kynneidai	²2871 (restored)	arch. 100/99	Pr. Apollo, tragic poet	
155	Kallimachos of Leukonoe	Keryx	MB_9	basileus	M1, M2, orator decreti, HA, Supt. Delos, HG, thesmothetes	'Princeps Atheniensium' from this family (Cic. *Fam.* 16.21.5)
157	Timotheos of Kephisia	?Keryx	$?MB_{11,25}$	thesmothetes		like roots only; speculative
158	Dositheos of Myrrhinoutta	?Sal.	?²3488	"	treas. of annona, Supt. Delos, thesmothetai	Dau. *arrephoros* of Pandrosos; priestess is Amyn.

Line	Name	Genos	Evidence	Post Held thesmothetes	Other Posts in Family *epi bomoi* hierophant, hierophantis	Remarks
159	Menander of Paiania	Eum., Keryx	^{2}398$^{4/5}$			commercial interests: ^{2}287^2, ^{2}295^2
194	Argeios of Trikorynthos	Keryx	MB_{19}	archon	*epi ta hiera.* Peir. gen'l.	Pythais 'from Kerykes,' 106/5
195	Archonides s. of Naukratos of Kerameikos	Keryx	*FdD* III 2.13 II$_{11}$	basileus, 98/7	*epi ta hiera*	
202	Lakrateides I of Ikaria (PA 8970)	Eum.	Isae. 7.9	thesmothetes	Priest, Eleusis	hierophant *ca.* 353a.
223	?D]o[si]theos s. of Charias	?Sal.	*AJA* 49 (1945) 434	Supt. Peiraieus	agoranomos, *epi ta hiera* treas. of pryt.	Brother or other rel. has dau. priestess of Pandrosos
227	[Charias] s. of Charias of Aithalidai	Sal.	"	admiral		"
232	—pos s. of Philokrates of Phyle	?Ker.	*FdD* III 2.-13$_{12}$, 10$_{26}$	—	supts., choregos	like roots only; speculative

Line	Name	Genos	Evidence	Post Held	Other Posts in Family	Remarks
259	Zenon s. of Ariston of Marathon	Erysichthonides, Keryx, Geph.	*Hesperia* 9 (1940) 86 no. 17; *IdD* 1674 bis; $MB_{7,21}$	thesmothetes	archon, HG, Pr. Apollo, theoros, gynasiarch	triple gentile affiliation

46. The chief evidence for Keryx predominance is extrapolations from the *Mélanges Bidez* decree. Twenty-eight persons petition the demos to honor the daidouchos Themistokles. The first eight held specified office within the genos. The crux is the last twenty. Of these, nine can be proved to be gennetai, and of the nine, eight are Kerykes, or connected with the clan by adoption or marriage:

Line	Name	Evidence
20	Diotimos s. of Diodoros II of Halai	Mover of decree; therefore probably Keryx. But also envoy of Gephyraioi to Delphi: *Hesperia* 9 (1940) 86 no. 17.
21-2	Sarapion s. of Diokles of Melite	Father adopted a Keryx, Eudemos s. of Gorgippos of Melite (see *FdD* III 2.59, 74). S. himself brother-in-law of Medeios; his brother is Diokles of Melite in stemma *PA* 2, p. 82.
22	Diokles s. of Diokles of Melite	Daughter married Themistokles II, daidouchos, stemma [23510].
23	Themistokles s. of Xenokles of Hagnous	*MB* p. 829. Probably a brother of Theophrastos II, to be added to stemma, [23510].

88

Line	Name	Evidence
23–24	Dionysodoros s. of D. of Deiradiotai	Brother adopted by a Philotas of Sounion whose homonymous descendant was Herald of Areiopagus, $med.s.i.$ ([2]3540). Dittenberger ($Hermes$ 20 [1885] 1–40, esp. 36) argues these Heralds were Kerykes by genos. A Dionysios s. of Dionysodoros is listed as Erysichthonid at Delphi in 97/6: FdD III 2.10$_{18}$.
25	Demostratos s. of Dionysios of Pallene	Father is Herald of the Goddesses (Demeter and Kore) MB_8.
26–7	Aristaichmos s. of Ammonios of Anaphlystos	MI 150/49. Symbol two torches: daidouchos.
27	Sophokles s. of Philotas of Sounion	See on Dionysodoros of Deiradiotai, above, on lines 23–4.
28	Iophon s. of Dionysodoros of Sounion	See on Dionysodoros of Deiradiotai, above, on lines 23–4. These three all cherished some connection with Sophokles the tragic poet, especially through his devotion to the healing gods, Asklepios and Amynos: see [2]4447 ($post\ med.s.ii\ a.$).

If the arguments that the above are Kerykes seem persuasive, the same should apply by analogy to Seleukos s. of Demeas of Halae, MB_{30}, a descendant of the Demeas cited in the last note, line 24, and indeed to the other eleven petitioners, clansmen petitioning to honor one of their fellows.

47. [2]1036 (108/7: few gennetai), [2]1034 (103/2: many gennetai), [2]1942 and 1943 ($ca.$ 100):

Reference	Ergastine	Father	Genos	Evidence
1036 I_{43}	lost	Kallias of Bate	Eupatridai	Stemma *PA* I, p. 22. 3 brothers
1036 II_{44}	Mneso	Asklepiades of Berenikidai	Eteoboutadai	$^{2}6232$ *FdD* III 2.13 (106/5)
1036 I_{34}	Lysistrate	Mikion of Kephisia	"	23477
1034 I_{11}	Philotera	Nikomachos of Cholargos	"	23474
1034 II_{21}	[Dionysia]	Dion]ys[ios of Pallene]	Keryx	See *HSCP* 51 (1940)$_{147}$. 4 brothers
1034 I_{23}	Akestion	Xenokles of Acharnai	Keryx	Daidouchos: $MB_{40, 52}$; $^{2}3510$.
1034 I_{25}	Ktesikleia	Apollonios of Acharnae	Eumolpid	23487
1034 II_{5}	Megiste	Zenon of Marathon	Erysichthonidai Gephyraioi	*HSCP* 51 (1940)$_{259}$. 3 brothers
1942_{10}	Mikion	Miltiades of Lakiadai	Philaid	Marcellinus. *Vit. Thuc.* 3.
1034 I_{19}	Kleo	Nikias of Thorikos	?Euneidai	$^{2}2360_{4}$; *FdD* III 2.13$_{14}$
1034 I_{12}	Apollonia	Chairion of Hermos		
1034 I_{22}	Dameion	Agon of Phyle	[Apheida]ntidai *FdD* III 2.30 (106/5)	
1034 I_{28}	Atheno	Epaminondas of Perithoidai		
1943_{16-18}	[Theodora] [Apollodora] [Sosandra]	Sarapion of Melite (possibly also mover of $^{2}1036$)	Keryx	*HSCP* 51 (1940)$_{50}$. 2 brothers
1034 II_{9}	Panarista	Mantias of Marathon	?Salaminios	*HSCP* 51 (1940)$_{158}$; $^{2}3488$ (*arrephoros*); see n. 25 above

48. *HA* 437ff. Ferguson's narrative of the Sullan sack and its antecedents (435–459) is brilliant.

49. Durrbach, *Choix* nos. 99, 100 (to Mithridates V); nos. 113, 133–136 (to Mithridates VI). No. 137 is a dedication by Mithridates to Sarapis.

50. $^2 1713_{9-11}$.

51. Poseidonios ap. Athenaios 212B ff., a malicious account brilliantly translated by Ferguson, *HA* 441–444.

52. $^2 1713_{14}$.

53. M. Thompson, *New Style Coinage*, 425.

54. $^2 4103$.

55. $^2 4104$.

56. $^2 1039_{57}$. Mitsos has a new fragment including an Ammonios s. of Demetrios of Anaphlystos.

57. $^2 1035$, reading with Kahrstedt, ἀ[ναρχίαν] for ἀ[πόδοσιν] in line 19.

58. *Choix*, no. 152 = *Syll.*³, 681 = *IdD* 1604 *bis*, dated *ca.* 85. But no such proconsul is known at that date; perhaps it is the praetor of 71: F. Münzer (*RE* 3 [1899] s.v. 'Caecilius 74'). For Protimos' father see n. 45, line 158.

59. *IdD* 1955; above, n. 45, line 147.

60. *IdD* 1893, 2161, 2205; above, n. 45, line 155.

61. *IdD* 1093, dated by the Roman consul A. Flaminius, a significant innovation.

62. $^2 4105$. The demos dedicated on the Akropolis a statue of his daughter: $^2 4233$.

63. $^2 4104$.

64. $^2 3218$.

65. *IdD* 1621.

66. $^2 3429$.

67. $^2 1340$, 1095; $^2 3490$–3492.

68. $^2 1716$; *Hesperia* 9 (1940) 86, no. 17.

69. $^2 4109$.

70. *Hesperia* 10 (1941) 65 no. 31; republished *SEG* 21 (1965) 171 no. 494.

71. $^2 4704$, 3490. Stemma, Wilhelm, *Beiträge zur griechischen Inschriftenkunde* (Vienna 1909) 85. Honors to an ancestor, Oinophilos (*PA* 11364, *ca.* 100): *Hesperia* 33 (1964) 193 no. 43.

72. $^2 1716$, $^2 1713$.

73. *Ibid.*; stemma $^2 3595$.

74. $^2 1046$; stemma, *PA* 1361, cf. MB_{20-21}.

75. $^2 1717$. Metrodoros: above, n. 45, line 28; Eudemos: see MB_{15}.

76. Stemma *RE* (1937) s.v. Oinophilos (Raubitschek), Sp. 2255. An ancestor (Kallikratides II in the stemma) on a fourth-

century mortgage stone: *Hesperia* 32 (1963) 43 no. 52.

77. *Choix* no. 162: the demos and Pompeiastai dedicate a statue of Pompey to Apollo. Lucan 3.181–183; Caes. *B.Civ.* 3.5.1.

78. App. *B.Civ.* 2.88. An ephebe inscription of *ca.* 43/2 (*Hesperia* 34 [1965] 255–272 = ²1040 with new fgs.) shows activity not very different from that in 127/6 (see n. 35 above. The demilitarized young men listen to lectures and make a gift of 100 books to the gymnasion library. Reinmuth ("Attic Archons," *BCH* 90 [1966] 93–100) would date the stone 48/7.

79. *IdD* 1787 (*Choix* no. 166); above, n. 45, line 147.

80. ²3222/3.

81. *Fam.* 4.5.4 from Sulpicius Rufus, to console him on Tullia's death; ruined state possibly exaggerated.

82. *IdD* 1622.

83. *Choix* no. 168 (*ca.* 43). Hortensius was the son of the famous orator.

84. ²4111 (*ca.* 45); Cic. *Fam.* 4.12 J. H. Oliver (*AJP* 68 [1947] 150, 160) would date the inscription in the reign of Tiberius.

85. ²4110; ²4113.

86. ²1961; Diotimos son of Diodoros of Halai, line 3 (first in Kekropis); Sophokles son of Theophrastos of Hagnous, line 19 (second in Attalis).

87. ²1043$_{23-24}$. And his wife Octavia as Athena Polias, according to Raubitschek, *TAPA* 77 (1946) 146–50. Meritt would date the inscription 37/6.

88. M. Junius Silanus: ²4114.

89. *Hesperia* 8 (1939) 80 no. 26 (superseding ²1096). Mentioned are Theophilos III (*NPA* 56) and Diotimos, sons of Diodoros II of Halai, and Pammenes, son of Zenon of Marathon. Diotimos is Bouzyges and Priest of Zeus *en Palladioi*. Theophilos' homonymous grandfather was hieropoios on Lemnos in 75/4: *ASAA* n.s. 5, vol. 3/4 (1941/42) 84. Base of a statue dedicated by Pammenes: *Hesperia* 30 (1961) 247 no. 45.

90. *IdD* 1588 = *Choix* no. 171.

91. ²4116.

92. ²3173. Hoplite-general, Pammenes son of Zenon of Marathon; priestess, Megiste daughter of Asklepides of Halai.

93. P. Graindor, *Athènes sous Auguste* (Cairo 1927); *Athènes de Tibère à Trajan* (*ibid.* 1931): *Athènes sous Hadrien* (*ibid.* 1934); *Un milliardaire antique: Hérode Atticus et sa famille* (*ibid.* 1930).

94. "Here present are men from Athens, where men think humanity, learning, religion, grain, equity, and laws were born, and whence they were spread through all the earth. For the possession

of their city—because of its beauty—even the gods contended, as the story goes. It is of such antiquity that it produced, so they say, its people from its own soil, and the same land is their mother, their nurse, and their country. It has, moreover, such renown that the now shattered and weakened name of Greece is supported by the reputation of this city." *Pro Flacco* 62 (Loeb translation).

Index of *Gennetai* by *Genê*

Alphabetical Index of *Gennetai*

Index of *Gennetai* by *Genê*

Alphabetical Index of *Gennetai* Mentioned

(for details see under the appropriate *genos*)